Why Don't You Send Somebody?

Sermons For Advent,
Christmas, Epiphany
Cycle B First Lesson Texts

Frederick C. Edwards

CSS Publishing Company, Inc.
Lima, Ohio

WHY DON'T YOU SEND SOMEBODY?

Library of Congress Cataloging-in-Publication Data

Edwards, Frederick C., 1932-
    Why don't you send somebody? : sermons for Advent, Christmas, and Epiphany. First lesson / by Frederick C. Edwards.
        p.   cm.
    ISBN 1-55673-611-8
    1. Advent sermons. 2. Christmas sermons. 3. Epiphany season — Sermons. 4. Sermons, American. 5. United Methodist Church (U.S.) — Sermons. 6. Methodist Church — Sermons. 7. Bible. O.T. — Sermons. 8. Common lectionary (1992) I. Title.
BV40.E29   1993
252'.61—dc20
                                                                93-19941
                                                                CIP

9336 / ISBN 1-55673-611-8

To my mother, Marie Metz Edwards, and in memory of my father, Frederick C. Edwards, Sr., both of whom first led me in the Way; and to Marion Jackson McLean, and in memory of the Rev. Baron A. McLean, with thanks to Janet, their daughter and my wife.

Table Of Contents

Foreword

Fred Edwards has had a remarkable preaching ministry, and this collection of sermons is a fresh example of that ministry. This series of sermons prepared for Advent, Christmas and Epiphany in 1993-1994, combines a genuinely scholarly approach with an ability to illustrate points vividly. The illustrations are most always contemporary and invariably compelling. At the same time, the sermons are biblically based and are faithful to the themes of the unfolding Christian year.

In a time when preaching appears to many to be neglected and even in decline, it is heartening to read these sermons of a preacher who clearly gives time to his craft. Yet the sermons do not end up as purely "literary pieces," but exude a warmth and passion which cries out for them to be preached to a live and receptive congregation.

I hope this book will be read and absorbed by both clergy and laity. It demonstrates once again the immeasurable possibilities of preaching.

Jack M. Tuell
Bishop, retired
The United Methodist Church

Why Don't You
Send Somebody?

In the entrance of the magnificent modern cathedral of St. Michael in Coventry, England, a most enigmatic statement is emblazoned upon the floor in large gleaming brass letters that demand to be read. There is no escaping it, for one has to walk over it to enter the nave. It says, "TO THE GLORY OF GOD THIS CHURCH BURNT, NOVEMBER 14, 1941."

The incredible irony of that statement is what grabs the attention. "To the glory of God?" How can that be? That's the kind of statement one inscribes under a stained glass window or some other thing of beauty. How can it be said about the ruin of a beautiful cathedral? The ruins of tragedy are there for anyone to see. There beside the new ultra-modern cathedral is the burnt-out shell of the once glorious medieval gothic church burned to the ground by fire bombs during the wartime air raid. That was certainly no "act of God," nor was the destruction of that great church viewed at that time as in the most remote sense "to the glory of God." It was indeed a tragedy mourned not only by that city and the English people, but by people around the world. The work and skill and devotion and artistry that had taken generations to produce that glorious edifice took only one night to destroy. Its spectral ruins remain, left as an awesome mute reminder of what happens when we wander so far from God. The cathedral

9

was only part of the destruction of course. Factories and homes and lives were lost in that horrendous night of fire-bombing.

How then could anyone say, "To the glory of God this church burnt?" One of the vergers of the new cathedral provided an answer. He said that had it not been for the tragic destruction and what followed it, "we would have just one more old cathedral, beautiful to be sure, but probably not well used at all except to be visited by tourists." But because of the notoriety of what happened there, Coventry Cathedral has become an ecumenical center for peace and mutual understanding of people. Thousands of Christians representing many denominations and people of other faiths speaking a variety of languages come to Coventry to pray and work for world peace, to the end that such wanton destruction of life and beauty will cease and people will learn at last to live together peacefully and unafraid. No, it was not the destruction, but what was called forth out of the ashes and rubble that was to glorify God. It was the work of that great church that was transformed and refined, beginning with that terrible fiery night.

The reading from the 64th chapter of Isaiah is from the portion that Bible scholars call Trito-Isaiah. It is of unknown authorship, probably even the product of several minds, but certainly from sometime around 520 B.C.E., not yet 70 years after another time of war's destruction. Some were still alive who remembered the devastating fall of Jerusalem to the Babylonian armies and the terrible destruction that followed. The burned ruin of the once glorious temple built by Solomon was still not restored and stood as a gaunt reminder of defeat and destruction and of people taken off into bondage in a foreign land.

The ruined temple was symbolic of a deeper devastation. Three generations after that defeat those who had returned from Babylonia discovered they escaped captivity in a foreign land only to find themselves now captive to their own devastated land. It was a time of sadness, and of dejected and empty spirits. There was no inspiration among the people. None discerned a sign from God, and the situation seemed hopeless.

Into this hapless context came a prophetic voice speaking and writing in the name of the prophet Isaiah who two centuries before had challenged his people and called and even goaded them to courage and faith and godliness. This "Third Isaiah" appeals to Yahweh to repeat the wonders of the time of the exodus. Recalling how the people were led out from that earlier time of bondage in Egypt, when Yahweh made himself known in the quaking and smoking mountain, the prophets pray, "O that you would rend the heavens and come down . . ." Do it all again, Lord! Do something new with us. Make something of this mess, this rubble, this empty people!

The burned stones of Solomon's temple, some of which still stand and are today called the "Wailing Wall," and Coventry's now useless flying buttresses and empty window traceries that once held jewel-like glass are but symbols of the disasters that pervade and devastate the human spirit, and from which one must seek to rise again. Let's face it, living among the ruins can be pretty grim!

A friend who, as a child, lived in Berlin in 1945 still remembers that she literally breathed the destruction in the dust of shattered concrete and stone that was everywhere. It was on every surface, in clothing, in the air one breathed and the food and water that one consumed. As ubiquitous as the dust was, the depressing reality of the devastation that was impossible to escape. People walked around as in a nightmare, hollow-eyed and demoralized in the midst of that once beautiful city.

You see, the victims are always individuals, not groups. Tragedy is always specific in its effect upon people. One does not have to have been the victim of war or violence, or an outside force or enemy, to understand the desolation of the human spirit. The social ills we can all name do not just affect nameless and faceless groups. They are not statistical tables, but people who have the spirit crushed out of them by poverty, and unemployment, and racism. Whole sections of our society suffer together from these scourges, but it is individual people who are hurt by them.

11

There are also personal tragedies that befall individuals in the course of life that often are not shared with anyone else, when beautiful dreams come crashing down around one's ears and all that is left are the stark reminders living amidst the ruins of happier times, but which are now haunted with tragedy, as when every breath is heavy with the memory of loss of a husband or wife, or a child, or beloved parent. For others that personal tragedy may be the pain of divorce, or life wracked by addiction or violence. Or one may suddenly find the future and financial security threatened by failing health, or possessions and home swept away by natural disaster. No act of God, these tragedies, but it is difficult to shake off captivity to them, or see any way out. And inwardly the question is asked, "How will I be able to go on?" Some, reaching out from faith, and others crying out in desperation, turn to God for help.

Where is God when we sit among the ruins? Frequently we hear the expression of anger and bitterness, "O God, why did you let this happen to me?" God often gets the blame for the wreckage that happens in life. When tragedy is no one's fault there seems no way to explain it except to blame God. But God is not the culprit. A more cogent conclusion is that God is the One who helps a person do something creative with what is left. It is God who calls forth something new from the ash heap. It is God who helps us transform the rubble of destruction.

The Isaiah scripture was addressed to people who were immersed in the deep dark night of the human soul. They had all but given up on any help from the Lord. In fact no one was even calling upon the name of the Lord or reaching out to take hold of the hand that could lead them through their wilderness. We can understand some of that feeling, for sometimes in the depths of our own struggles we may have felt alone, and even that God is remote from us. That is the very feeling of those who sat amidst Jerusalem's ruins. But the prophetic word of hope to them suggests another prayer, "O that you would rend the heavens and come down!" Lord, do it all again!

12

Mark's gospel for the first Sunday in Advent records Jesus telling his followers to be alert and watchful for the coming of the Son of Man. "It will be like a man who goes away from home on a trip and leaves his servants in charge, each with his own work to do; and he tells the doorkeeper to keep watch." (Mark 13:32ff) The watchfulness he describes is not mere idleness, but the work of faithfulness and discipline. God comes to those who watch expectantly; who do not give up or fall idle, or simply go to sleep. Those who anticipate the coming of the Lord do something to prepare. If Christ is to come once more to us we need to be watching and waiting. This season of Advent reminds us it is time to prepare. As we approach Christmas and read once again the familiar narratives of the nativity we may notice that the scriptures lead us to understand that most people in that time seemed unaware of the coming of Jesus. That quiet event was revealed only to those who watched and waited. This Advent season reminds us that God does indeed come to those who wait and watch and prepare.

We are the self-proclaimed servants of God. We are the ones whose work of preparation is to proclaim that God has indeed riven the heavens and come down among humankind in a very special way in Jesus.

God does not visit calamity upon us. Rather, God has already rent the skies and come down, and in Christ opened our eyes to what God is already doing in the world. Our transformation begins when we realize that whatever "testing by fire" we have been through we are not finished. We are just refined. God has still greater purposes for each of us than we yet realize.

All about us in the communities where we live are people sitting dejected among the ruins of some tragedy. For them life is heavy and painful and enfolded by gloom, and it seems as though there is no light of God breaking in upon that darkness. But for them we have a message. We must tell them, "Don't give up!" Dejected spirits are immobilizing and defeating. To those who hope for a word of encouragement or direction from God we need give them the unmistakable message of compassionate love we have seen in Jesus. If they have seen no light upon their situation then we must embody that light in ways and deeds that bring some very personal light into another's personal darkness. This is our work; the work of the church. This is our faithful and watchful preparation for the advent of Christ, to bring the love of God into people's lives now.

There is a wonderful story from rabbinic lore of a man who looked around at the world and was deeply distressed by what he saw. On every hand there was trouble and turmoil and exploitation. He saw people suffering in poverty and ignorance. There was pain and grief and anguish in their lives. So he cried out in prayer to God, "Lord, look at this world of yours. Look at what is going on. The world is in such a mess. There is so much misery and pain. Why don't you send somebody to help?" And to his surprise God answered and said, "I did. I sent you."

Advent 2
Isaiah 40:1-11

Comfort

"Comfort! Comfort my people, says your God." How
wonderful those words sound to us. How many times we feel
the need for comfort. How often we need an assuring and
tender word to ease the hurt we feel. Every year about this
time we hear those wonderful prophetic words sung in Han-
del's *Messiah*, or read in our churches from the portion of
scripture that biblical scholars call "Second Isaiah," to dis-
tinguish it from the writings of the eighth-century prophet.

They were written for a people for whom things had gone
terribly wrong. A terrible calamity had taken place. The nation had been overrun by the Babylonian armies in 587-86
B.C.E. Jerusalem was destroyed and laid waste and some
15,000 people were hauled off into captivity to a foreign land
hundreds of miles away across the desert to the region of
present-day Baghdad. There they were held against their will
in servitude to their captors for nearly 70 years, separated from
parents and children, husbands and wives, most never to see
each other again.

It was a long captivity. Few of the original captives lived
to return. Generations of children were born and grew up there
having only heard stories of the land from which their parents or grandparents had come. Through all those years the
idea of returning was kept alive. Jerusalem was still "home,"

15

though Babylonia probably seemed like home to those who had never known anything else, and who had found a place for themselves in that land. The desire to return to Jerusalem was by no means shared by all the exiles, but it remained an ardent and burning hope for many.

We all remember that time when hostages were being held somewhere in Lebanon. Some of them had been there for several years. Occasional pictures would be sent out by their captors to let the world know they were still alive and to keep the hurt festering. How our hearts ached for those men and for their families who longed to have them home again. We remember the feeling. How we and they needed the comfort that could only come by their release and return. Magnify that feeling several thousand times and you'll have an idea of the impact that captivity in Babylon had on the devastated and overrun land and the people who remained, and upon the captives who, like captives of any time, lived in hope of returning home someday. Most never did. "Comfort, comfort my people, says your God."

Some saw destruction and captivity as the punishing hand of God for Israel's unfaithfulness. To those the prophet said, "Speak tenderly to Jerusalem and cry to her that her warfare is ended, that her iniquity is pardoned, that she has received from the Lord's hand double for all her sins." (Isaiah 40:2)

Repentance for what one has done is a necessary factor of the biblical equation of forgiveness, but it needs to be worked to conclusion. One cannot live with guilt without end. Parents and children, husbands and wives frequently do not understand that and go on forever reminding that spouse or child or parent of some long-past sin of commission or omission. There has to be a time when we say "Enough! It's over!" "Comfort. Comfort my people. ... Cry to her ... that her iniquity is pardoned."

When Babylonian power began to fade, the Persians were expanding their empire and finally were ready to conquer Babylonia itself. A school of prophecy naming itself for the great eighth century prophet Isaiah, saw the opportunity to fuel the fires of hope exemplified in this magnificent 40th chapter of Isaiah. The prophetic task was to prepare the people to take advantage of their freedom when the opportunity should come, which meant the creation of a new state of mind among the exiles. The exiles had lost hope of a return and made up their minds to accept the inevitable and make the best of their lot.

The prophet's message grew out of this situation. It is a message of prevailing hope and encouragement and of a future glorious with the promise soon to be fulfilled. Nowhere is the omnipotence of Yahweh more eloquently or powerfully portrayed than in the words of this unknown prophet:

> *On a high mountain get you up,*
> *O heralds of good news to Zion!*
> *Lift up your voice with strength*
> *O heralds of good news to Jerusalem!*
> *Lift it up, fear not;*
> *Say to the cities of Judah,*
> *"Behold your God!"*
> — Isaiah 40:9

To those who waited and hoped and prayed for vindication, and for bondage to Babylon to be thrown off, the conquering armies of Persia seemed like instruments in the hand of the Lord. "See! The Lord God is coming with might, his own arm having won him the kingdom ...." The prophet's words did not simply lift up the possibility that they could soon be going home. Indeed it was stated as a certainty. How's that for a comforting word to captives? "Free at last! Free at last! Great God A'mighty, I'm free at last!" But becoming free is not usually an easy matter — not just a matter of walking out and being free. There is always a price for freedom. The Hebrew exiles probably thought they'd paid it all, but listen to the Prophet's word:

> *In the wilderness prepare the way of the Lord, make*
> *straight in the desert a highway for our God. Every valley*

*shall be lifted up, and every mountain and hill be made
low; the uneven ground shall become level and the rough
places a plain. And the glory of the Lord shall be revealed
and all flesh shall see it together, for the mouth of the
Lord has spoken.*

— Isaiah 40:3-5

The way home was to be across the desert, in the fastest
and most direct way possible. That was the price. Don't waste
time going the longer and easier way up the Euphrates River
and down from the north. Take the risk! Seize the day!

To understand the price of such a journey take a look at
a map of that region between Jerusalem and Babylonia. Draw
a straight line between them and see what the terrain is like.
You may remember seeing pictures from the time of the Gulf
War depicting the harshness of the desert. Between Babylon
and Jerusalem were hills and valleys, sandy desert and rough
ground — intense heat in the summer and bitter cold in the
winter. That might be difficult enough for the young and able-
bodied, but would you take old men and women, and children, and expectant mothers on a trip like that, plus everything they'll need to survive? That's insane! That's enough to
give one some second thoughts because it sounds more like
aggravation than comfort. But then do we really understand
comfort?

Comfort, in an old and largely obsolete definition, means
"to make one strong." That certainly has more meaning here
than the ease and relaxation that we might better describe as
"comfy." "To be made strong." Is that one of the ways our
prayers are answered?

On a very personal level, a great many of our prayers concern illness. How earnestly we pray to "change" that situation of illness for ourselves or someone else. What we want
is for it to go away, but it doesn't usually happen that way.
Certainly there are occasional spontaneous remissions or
reversals of illness, but it is highly questionable that they occur
because we have mounted a prayer campaign and convinced

God to change the situation. There are miracles wrought by prayer nevertheless — the miracle of strengthening being one of the most important. Think of how wonderful it is to make persons strong enough to bear whatever are the burdens of their lives. That kind of miracle happens all the time. Some of you know about that from personal experience because it has happened to you.

To be strong to bear one's burdens doesn't sound like much of a miracle. Comfort doesn't mean the situation will become easy. The alcoholic will still have to take it one day at a time. Living the rest of our lives without a loved one who has died will not be easy. Coping with a disability, bearing pain, loving someone who is hard to love are all difficult to do. They require strength often beyond our limits. But there is reassurance — tender reassurance. "Don't be afraid . . . . Behold, your God comes with strength, . . . and reward . . . and vindication. . . . He will feed his flock like a shepherd, he will gather the lambs in his arms. And he will carry them in his bosom, and gently lead those that are with young." (Isaiah 40:9-11)

Five centuries after the time of this Second Isaiah, John the Baptist appeared in the desert at a place along the Jordan River and proclaimed the good news about Jesus in some of the very same words: "Prepare the way of the Lord. Make a straight way in the desert for him." Like the prophet of old he urged people to make a venture of faith. If we want the comfort of God we need to prepare for it. We always need to prepare for whatever we want to happen in life or we find ourselves simply drifting along without direction or purpose, and frustrated much of the time.

There are hills and valleys and rough places in our lives that are barriers to God working in any of us and they need to be leveled and smoothed. They may be rocky relationships or strained or broken friendships. They may be stormy tempers that flare and moody valleys that are unpredictible and hazardous. We need to take charge of whatever it is that produces the turmoil and pressure and anxiety within us. Is there substance dependence that needs to be admitted is out of control? There is no better time than now to begin to work on straightening out a disordered and aimless lifestyle that encourages us to wander off into unfulfilling byways.

Here we are in the season of Advent preparing for Christmas. We can just decorate the exterior and cover up what is underneath, or we can make some substantive changes that will smooth the way for the God-presence to come into our lives in a special way this year. We can take a venture of faith and discover the inner strength that is true comfort in the midst of whatever distress or turmoil we may find ourselves. And we may find to our surprise that the God who chose to become known in the Child of Bethlehem will choose to be born anew in our hearts and minds.

"Comfort, give comfort to my people," says the ancient but contemporary prophetic voice. "And the glory of the Lord shall be revealed, and we shall see it together."

Send Me!

Certain events — often cataclysmic ones — stand out in bold relief in our memory. Those of you who are over 35 or so, think of where you were or what you were doing when you heard the news that President John Kennedy had been shot. You may not remember the date — it was November 22, 1963 — but you will probably remember other things about that day. Or if you are 60 or more think of what you were doing when you learned that Pearl Harbor had been attacked. Chances are some things about that day are etched clearly in your memory. People who were in the region of San Francisco on that fateful day in November, 1989, will always remember that the ground shook and freeways collapsed and buildings crumbled. Chances are that people on the eastern coast of the United States will never forget the days at the end of October, 1991, when the fiercest storm anyone could recall battered the towns and harbors along the waterfront. Certainly the residents of southern Florida will never forget Hurricane Andrew, that laid waste to Dade County and cut a swath across the state. Of course the events that stick in our memory don't need to be tragic ones. They may be joyful ones. Landing on the moon! The Berlin Wall coming down. The end of a war, and knowing that a loved one is coming home. A wedding. The birth of a child. We all mark our lives by key events of our history and by the fortunes or struggles, the triumphs or tragedies that we share together or in our families. Our lives are shaped to some degree by those events.

The early life of the prophet Isaiah was shaped by the events of his own time. Little wonder then that he dates his vision in the Temple by the time when the great King Uzziah died. Uzziah began his reign in 783. He became king when he was only six years old, and he ruled for almost 50 years as a great and good king. He ruled so long that the fortunes of the nation and the rule of Uzziah almost seemed as one. He developed the nation's agriculture. Throughout his reign there was prosperity in the land. His leadership inspired his people. He raised a mighty army and strengthened the walls of Jerusalem against attack from without. Under his leadership the nation prevailed against the Philistines and the Arabians. It was a good time for the country and for the people. But the king became ill with leprosy, and his death was charged with great emotion throughout the country. Imagine the sorrow and the sudden uncertainty about the future among the people, most of whom had never known another king.

Now, imagine an aristocratic young man named Isaiah who admired that king, and may even have known him. The king's death and the nation in mourning formed the background of the call of God to Isaiah to do something special with his life. It was in the temple — the one built long before by King Solomon — that Isaiah envisioned "the Lord high and lifted up, and his train filled the temple." He realized that he was in the very presence of God, and confessed his unworthiness to be there. The sacrifice was there burning upon the altar, and Isaiah's vision was that one of the guardians of the throne of God touched his lips with the fire as a sign of his purification. Then Isaiah heard the Lord ask, "Whom shall I send? Who will go for us?" And perhaps to his own amazement Isaiah found himself answering, "Here I am, Lord. Send me."

What a wonderful story! That powerful vision had a profound impact upon a young man who probably would otherwise have chosen a much easier and conventional and less controversial life. But the biblical story, the historical record and our own times reveal that those who encounter the presence of God in their own lives can never be the same. It is clear that Isaiah believed himself called by God to be something very special. He could never live the privileged and pampered life to which he had been born. He was changed.

Change is not always easy to accommodate, either in ourselves or by those around us. Several years ago there was a film called *The Subject Was Roses*. It portrayed a young man who returned home from the army only to discover that he was a different person than the boy who had left three years before. He was mature and independent — his own man. And the difference between what he had been and what he had become ignited an intense conflict in the family. His parents didn't know how to respond to this young man. Because he had changed, they had to change, too. The whole family structure began to fall apart. And the son, realizing that he was the focus of their pain, could not stay. He had to leave.

How we want people to stay the same. We don't reason that out, of course, but somehow we assume it. Children grow up and become independent. They do not want to be directed by their parents as they were when they were younger. The child must eventually put away being a child and become the self-directed adult, thinking and acting in adult ways. That is the very thing for which good parenting prepares a child, but the parents sometimes have difficulty adjusting to that when it happens. A husband or wife takes on new interests, grows into new ideas and attitudes, while the other does not. Suddenly one or the other wakes up and says, "Is this the same person I married?" Relationships feel the strain, and unfortunately some marriages do not survive the stress. We encounter friends of years ago, and while we remember there was a time we shared together, we discover we no longer have much in common. Have they changed, or have we? Change is not always easy to accept. At least we seem to want it on our own terms. But change happens, and sometimes in radical fashion. Sometimes growth comes in great leaps.

The biblical record is rife with such changes initiated by the insistent call of God in one's life. Moses was called from being a shepherd in a foreign land to lead his people to freedom. Zacchaeus, upon meeting Jesus, changed from being a cheat and became an honest man. Saul, the persecutor of Christians, became Paul the Apostle of Jesus. And the young Isaiah was changed from the comfortable aristocrat to become the fiery prophet of God.

Certainly many of the disciples had radical changes wrought in their lives upon meeting Jesus. Levi, who had become wealthy as a tax collector, exchanged material comfort for the life of an itinerant disciple. And two pairs of brothers who were fishermen gave up catching fish to catch people. In fact the scripture for today puts it this way, "They gave up everything and followed him."

If we were able to ask Simon when that great change took place in his life, or James or John, they might say, "It was when we took that tremendous catch of fish. Remember? Never had we caught so many at once. Our boats were about to sink with the weight of them." Luke seems to credit Jesus with the miraculous catch, but they all surely regarded it as a sign from God. Fear seized them and they felt unworthy to be in Jesus' presence. Jesus told them not to be afraid, but to follow him and henceforth to catch people.

Was it easy for those about them? Perhaps not. It is never pleasant to be left behind. There was uncertainty, and later on conflict, and at the end death. Matthew's account tells of James and John leaving rather precipitously with their father Zebedee sitting there in the boat, probably amazed and bewildered. How could they leave him without help? Who could replace them? How is that for parental frustration with change? We know very little of the effect upon wives and children and parents, but certainly there must have been some who were skeptical of the whole idea, if not outright angry. We can project that because those are the very feelings people have today when some radical change occurs. Most of us resist the changes that reshape those who are close to us.

There is indeed a skepticism about change in people's lives. Perhaps many of us view with some doubt the kind of jailhouse conversions that seem to be ploys to get off a bit easier. Undoubtedly that is true in some instances, but is our view so jaundiced that we doubt that God can and does touch the lives of people who have gotten into desperate circumstances? It is possible that the shock of the realization of the depth to which one's life has fallen may even be the key to open the human mind and soul to the only chance left — the chance that God offers.

Do you remember Watergate conspirator Chuck Colson? He went to prison for his part in that political debacle. And while he was there it was reported that he had experienced a religious conversion, and that as a result his life was changed. A news correspondent in Washington at the time reflected the cynicism of many others when he said, "If Chuck Colson has been washed in the blood of the Lamb, then he has 'ring around the collar.' "[1] But whatever one may think of his part in political shenanegans and crimes, or the theological perspective he now represents, whatever happened seems to be a permanent change. He has been writing and speaking of the change Christ has wrought in his life ever since that day. In the year of Watergate it happened, in the shadow of events that shook a nation. A man found himself uncomfortable in the presence of God and begged forgiveness. "Whom shall I send? Who will go for us?" We who confess our skepticism must remember that it happened to Isaiah, and it happened to Paul. There were plenty who doubted the genuineness of his conversion, too.

Life cannot remain on dead center and still be regarded as life in the best sense. Life must be dynamic. It must move. It can only go forward. We can never turn back the clock, or go back to what we once were. To stand still is to die, or at least to miss out on the life that God offers us. We all must grow, and to grow is to outgrow the past and even the present and to embrace the new. The opportunity comes to each one of us, in different ways certainly. But we all are led forward to be what God has created us to be. God can speak to and within us, perhaps not with overwhelming visions, but certainly with a larger vision than we have created for ourselves. We raise the question, "Why me?" because we feel afraid or unworthy. Don't forget Isaiah. And don't forget Simon either, called to discipleship while caught in the midst of pulling fish into a boat. They both felt unworthy and afraid. Don't be afraid. Jesus said that too, remember? Don't be afraid. Answer the call. Open up your life to the new thing God is about to do with your life. God's will for us only happens with our cooperation.

Might God be calling you from too self-indulgent a lifestyle to one of helpful concern for the plight of people less fortunate than yourself? Might God be calling you from isolation from the world to involvement in real life? Is God asking you to encourage those who because of handicap or poverty struggle against overwhelming odds? Do you hear a still small but insistent voice saying, "Whom shall I send to teach little children and to guide young lives?" Have you said no too many times to opportunities to be used by God? Maybe it is time you began to say yes.

What is the call in your life? Is it to be more generous with your time or money? Is it to hear the voices that challenge comfortable attitudes and subtle prejudices? Are the channels of communication open as you go about your daily routine, or as you do your work? In other words, do you pray? Not in the sense of asking, or forming prayers of words, but are you open and ready for God to speak to you in the experiences and people around you? Indeed are you open to the fact that this is the temple of God?

Even as we worship today we recognize God is present. We confess our feelings of unworthiness, and perhaps even our fear that God may ask something of us we are reluctant to do. It is natural to wonder where our yes is going to lead us, but then just how much do we trust God? In so many ways at this moment God is calling each one of us.

Life does not progress without change. Expect it! Be open to it. And welcome the change that God offers. Say it! "Here I am, Lord! Send me!"

———————

[1]Excerpt from *Good News*, © published by Liturgical Publications, Inc., 2875 S. James Drive, New Berlin, WI 53151. From a sermon written by Rev. Frederick C. Edwards.

Break Through

In the reading for today, King David calls the court prophet, Nathan, to him to propose a building project. David considers it unseemly that while he lives in a palace of paneled luxury, the ark of the covenant is still in a tent. Now the ark of the covenant, you should know, was a very important object. It was essentially a box, carved and decorated, and fitted with long pole-handles so it could be carried about from place to place as the people moved. It was important because it was the prime symbol of the covenant between God and the Israelites. The covenant and the tradition surrounding it trace back to the time of desert wandering accounted in the scriptures as Moses was leading the people out from slavery in Egypt.

We can only guess that the ark of the covenant contained some religious artifacts — perhaps writings like the 10 commandments and others of the laws that governed the people. But most important of all it was the symbol of the agreement between Yahweh and the people whereby God said, "If you will listen to my voice and do my will, then I will be your God, and you shall be my people." Of course there are always two parts to a covenant, and the people agreed, "All that God has said, we will do." Needless to say, then, the ark as a symbol of the identity of the people was very important.

But now the people were not going anywhere. They were no longer wanderers. They were settled down in towns and were growing crops. True, the ark of the covenant had been carried into battle, and it was assumed that so long as they kept possession of the ark they would be victorious. But most of the time the ark just sat there in its tent, as though ready to move on to the next place. So David now proposed to build a house for the ark.

Our scripture for today tells of a very interesting conversation that ensued that night between the prophet Nathan and the Lord, in which Nathan was told just exactly what to say to David. "Would you build me a house to dwell in?" says the Lord. It was not really a question to be answered, but one of incredulity on the part of the Lord.

> *"I have not dwelt in a house since the day I brought up the people of Israel from Egypt. I have been moving about in a tent for my dwelling. ... Did I ever complain?"*
>
> —2 Samuel 7:6-7, paraphr.

And the confusion in our minds as to whether this is a house for God or for the ark is, I think, central to the controversy. While David's idea of building a house — later called a temple — for the ark is a well intentioned idea, God does not need the house. Surely there was a concern that in the minds of the people the mere housing of that sacred reliquary would be mistaken as a residing place of God, as in some of the other indigenous religions of the area.

Then after reminding David of his call from being a shepherd boy to become a great king and rule over a people, there is a little play on words. "The Lord will make you a house." But the meaning of "house" has shifted. David spoke only of making a structure to house the ark of the covenant — to protect it from the weather and give it a more dignified and honorable place to be than in a dusty wind-blown tent. But God's word through Nathan was about something much more important than a building, to the point that God will establish his house — or his dynasty or family line — through the faith of David and his people. God will do it! David need only trust and be the willing servant.

> *I will raise up your offspring after you who shall come forth from your body, and I will establish his kingdom. He shall build a house for my name, and I will establish the throne of his kingdom forever. I will be his father and he shall be my son. And your house and your kingdom shall be made sure forever before me; your throne shall be established forever.*
> —2 Samuel 7:12b-13

As it happened it was David's offspring, Solomon, not David, who built the first Temple.

Perhaps David could not see the plan of God. Usually we cannot. Like David we are aware of our plans and goals, and in our own minds we tend to arrogate them to the status of divine purpose. But also like David, we are asked to trust and be willing servants.

The story in Samuel probably reflects a conflict in the perception of what the Hebrew people ought to be. David's idea suggests that a settled people ought to have a settled faith. The building of a temple suggests a more institutionalized religion, centered in a place — even a building — within a land which would be equated with the land of God's covenant promise. In a sense it was almost a throwback to the terrritorial God idea. And in a practical sense it seemed to work out that way, that the Israelites and later the Jews did tend to equate that real estate with the land of promise, and do even now, as attested to by many arguments put forth for Israel to be established in 1947 as the Jewish homeland. David, in proposing a temple, was proposing an idea that supported not just a religion centered in a place, but a mindset that had "settled," and in a very important sense had ceased its quest.

On the other hand there was the idea that the Israelites should always be a pilgrim people, and always be in quest of a land of promise that was not geographical, but mental and spiritual. The ark of the covenant still in the tent bespoke a people ready to move, in mind and spirit, if not physically, to find a higher righteousness, and to retain a freedom to serve the call of God.

We have a similar conflict in the church. There is always the tension between building a bigger edifice and serving the needs of the institution, and being free to move or to change to serve God in new ways as the occasion arrives. Perhaps the church needs to develop more of a tent mentality than a cathedral mentality, with freedom to pull up stakes and answer the call of God in a new place and a new way, and be a pilgrim people in quest of the kingdom of God.

The danger lurking in David's good intent was that the institution would harden and that God would have to break through settled traditions and fixed thought and rigid opinions to establish the tent mentality of a pilgrim people once again. The institution did harden. So does the church. And God has to continually break through in the thinking of a new thought or the enactment of a new idea. Jesus continually struggled against the aspects of Judaism that were "poured in concrete," but their reason for being had been forgotten. That always happens when people begin serving institutions instead of institutions serving people.

God's message through Nathan to David was no mere playing with words. It was a promise. It was the faithfulness of David, and others like him, that would be established. It was the lineage of faith that would become a "house" of God. And through the people of the house of faith God would continue to break into the history of humankind to put them on the move again to a land of promise and a kingdom of God. David's part was to trust, and be a willing servant. That is exactly what is asked of the house of faith today.

In this season we celebrate what we regard as the ultimate of break-throughs. Luke's gospel tells us how it began, with one of those trusting and willing servants, a young woman whose name is Mary. She is bethrothed to a man named

32

Joseph, who just happened to be part of the family descended from that now ancient king, David. It was probably an arranged marriage, as was the custom. Extra-biblical tradition holds that Joseph was considerably older than Mary. That often happened, too. A bride price was surely paid, and Mary may or may not have even seen this man, Joseph, whom she would marry. As she was nervously awaiting her marriage this disturbing angel visitation takes place. She is afraid, but she does not protest. Notice that she asks none of the "why me" questions. She only wants to know "how." In trust she gives her "yes" by saying, "I am the maidservant of the Lord. Let it be as you say."

Notice that her answer is not one of great confidence in her own fitness for her part, but one of trust that God does not ask the impossible of us. What we may ascribe to Mary as innocence we might better call obedience. A maidservant does what is asked of her. Asked, mind you, not demanded. She could have protested, carried on, cried and thrown a tantrum, but obediently she said "yes." With her affirmation the stage is set for God to break through to humankind in a most ordinary and yet most unexpected way; the birth of a child.

Have you ever wondered about the selection process for Mary? What I really wonder is if that angelic emissary of God had tried any others first. Was she top of the list, or perhaps third or fourth? Of course we do not know, but it is interesting to speculate that God's breakthrough might have been frustrated for a while by other young maids not so readily trusting as this one. And what if she had said "no?" What then? Would that have ended it all and changed the course of history? Would God have had to break through some other way? But what we do know is that this one was willing, and trusted. And she said yes.

I have never understood people who always seem to say no even to requests that are not very demanding. "I don't have time." Few of us have as much time as we want. "I don't have enough energy." Who has? "I wouldn't know what to do." Would anyone ever become a parent if they had to know all about child raising at the beginning rather than learning along the way? We don't know where our yes will lead, but then, do we ever? In marriage? In business? In the pursuit of any worthwhile adventure?

In fact most of our yeses are rather easy ones. They are because we have some confidence in those who ask, and who have confidence in us. In this Advent season we try to cultivate a fresh openness to the possibility that God has something for each of us to do. But God must break through to us before God can break through through us. Perhaps God needs each of us as a means of bringing new life to a church which has become insular and settled, and needs to get on the road again.

You see we are asked to trust that we can play a part in the purposes of God, and that there is an intent that the best in life will be furthered through us — but only if we are willing. Our willingness and trust are necessary to the fulfillment of God's intent. That's what this young woman did. The story Luke tells us shows no reasoning out of the possibilities, no weighing of the pros and cons, no indecision. She apparently instinctively trusted in the word from God. So, in time a child was born, and once again God broke through in something that seemed small and insignificant, at least as the world measures events. And because of Mary's willing trust the promise of God to the ancient shepherd-king, David, was fulfilled in a new time in the birth of Jesus. At least that's the way the gospel writer sees it. Do you remember the promise? "I will make YOU a house." God will make a house, more grand than any earthly temple, of the household of faith.

Could she have even suspected the magnitude of her role as an enabler of God's purpose? Surely not. Nor can we know the impact of our own part in the cause of God to which we are invited. We'll never be ready enough, wise enough, knowledgeable enough, have time enough, or energy or skill enough. But fortunately God usually invites us at the small end of the task. For some even that may be terrifying enough, but don't say no. Our part is to be the willing servant, and trust. That's faith.

The philosopher George Santayana's poem suggests the answer to our often too reluctant and hesitant faith.

O world, thou choosest not the better part!
It is not wisdom to be only wise,
And on the inward vision close the eyes,
But it is wisdom to believe the heart.

Our knowledge is a torch of smoky pine
That lights the pathway but one step ahead
Across a void of mystery and dread.
Bid, then, the tender light of faith to shine
By which alone the mortal heart is led
Unto the thinking of the thought divine.[1]

In six days Christmas is upon us once more. Christmas is God's affirmation that there is something about humanity worth saving and giving a most precious gift. It is the gift we call Emmanuel — God immanent — "God with us." It is a gift we can claim for ourselves every day of our lives and in every situation of life.

Inwardly we confess our sophisticated skepticism that God could or would do such a thing. Perhaps we question that the God who enlisted a shepherd boy to be king, and who enlisted a young bride to fulfill a promise to humankind, would seek to enlist us also. Possibly the greatest gift we can receive this year is the realization that God has some purposes in mind for each of us and is trying to break through to us. It is a good season to think about that, for somehow God seems closer and more real to us this season. And perhaps in the season of Emmanuel, God with us, each of us may discover a new trust within ourselves, and the courage to answer with a young maid named Mary, "Behold, I am the Lord's servant. Let it be done according to your word."

---

[1]Irwin Edman, ed., *The Philosophy of George Santayana.*

Just A
Whisper

A newborn child is such a small and fragile thing. Can it have the power to change anything?

In the eighth century B.C.E., Ahaz, King of Judah, faced the armies of two kings advancing to attack Jerusalem, and a state of mind bordering on panic seized the king and the people. Into that climate of fear came the prophet Isaiah, who met Ahaz one day as he was inspecting the water supply of Jerusalem in anticipation of the siege of the city. Isaiah called upon Ahaz to have unwavering faith in Yahweh, so that the kingdom would not fall. The sign Isaiah gave him was that a child would be born whose very name would be a reminder of God's constant presence — Emmanuel, God with us. But what difference could a child make, who could not even hold a weapon against the invading foe?

Ahaz put aside Isaiah's appeal and took the apparently more practical course. He appealed to the Assyrian king for help, and made himself and his people subservient to Assyria. Isaiah was not so impractical a dreamer as it might have seemed. Had faith in God stiffened Ahaz' resolve the disaster might not have happened — but it did. As it was Israel paid heavily for its reliance on Assyria. Heavy tribute was exacted. Rebels were punished. Much of Judah's territory was lost, and many people were deported to Assyria as slaves. But Isaiah was not through. Once again he stood forth and prophesied:

The people who walked in darkness have seen a great light; those who lived in a land of deep darkness, on them light has shined.

— Isaiah 9:2

He was telling the people that even though the kingdom had been ruined, there is a new freedom on the horizon when the Messiah is born, for he will bring peace and justice.

... A child has been born for us, a son given to us; authority rests upon his shoulders; and he is named Wonderful Counselor, Mighty God, Everlasting Father, Prince of Peace.

— Isaiah 9:6

How can all that be wrapped up in a child?

During the last week of August, 1989, the spacecraft, Voyager, sent back breathtaking pictures of the planet Neptune and its rings and moons. Though the news broadcasts gave it not much more time than national sports, the pictures sent from space to earth in those few days changed forever our concept of Neptune. Even the scientists who designed Voyager never dreamed what was going to be revealed. They knew the spacecraft would work for five or six years, fulfill its then intended mission, and lapse into silence never to be heard from again. But now we know its power supply will keep it operating for at least 28 years, and far beyond our solar system. Voyager's course has been given minute corrections along the way to its destination with such accuracy that it might be likened to a golfer putting a ball from the east coast and sinking it in Palm Springs.

Now think for a moment of how this miraculous information came to us. Spacecraft Voyager's voice is not a loud one — only 21 watts. But from 2.8 billion miles in space, requiring four hours to reach earth, its signal was only about one

20-billionth of the power required to run an ordinary electronic digital watch.

After Voyager had been launched and was already six or seven years into its voyage a new receiver was devised by scientists at General Electric. That receiver was hooked up to a dozen or so giant antennae near Socorro, New Mexico, linked together in a configuration that constituted an enormous signal-receiving dish, with a capability of receiving a signal from space as weak as 12-billionths of a billionth of a billionth of one watt! Now for you mathematicians, the way to write that would be 10 to the minus 28 (10^{-28} watts.) By anyone's standards that barely qualifies as even a whisper. But because of that faint whisper our understanding of the cosmos will never be the same. It was enough.

We're not usually tuned to receive such important whispers. As King Ahaz and his people waited for the sure destruction of Jerusalem, the word of the Lord came to them from the prophet Isaiah, with the promise that if they would just trust in Yahweh the city would not fall. Isaiah was hoping to turn the king and the people to faith, and to galvanize their resistance against the invaders. And this would be the validation of the promise, that a young woman would conceive and bear a child. It was a sign of almost laughable insignificance. What woman? What child? Besides, what meaning could the birth of any child have in the face of the might of two advancing armies? Can sure destruction be turned aside by the whisper of God? Yet in the midst of the terror of siege that little child's name would be a reminder — "Emmanuel!" God immanent! God present! God with us! The whisper would be enough.

It is amazing that God often gives people whispers of hope in the midst of desperate times. Fifty years ago the Nazi armies besieged Leningrad for 900 days. Virtually every building was destroyed. People lived through bitter cold and near starvation. They slept in basements, in the shelter of destroyed walls, and in shells of shattered buildings. For months they lived on nothing but a small handful of bread per day. Still they resisted the massive power of the German army. Amazing though it seems, in the midst of that destruction and death there were still some babies being born. How ridiculous that seems! What a world to bring a little child into. Didn't those people know they were going to die? Didn't they know there was no hope? So what is the meaning of a child being born? For destruction and death? No, because even in the midst of that terror there was reason to hope for life. It seems the Creator has endowed humankind with a bit of the Divine nature, by which hope is born anew to bring light into the darkness of despair. Perhaps some would argue, saying, "But most of those were probably non-believers! How can you say that God was doing that?" Simply because belief — or non-belief — is a perspective of humankind. The perspective of God must still be the constant affirmation of life. And whether we recognize it or not, new life is the most eloquent sign of the presence of God.

The promised sign wasn't enough for Ahaz. It is not enough for many people today, and hence we put our trust in might and power. The sign of God's love in Jesus may seem every bit as ineffective as we face our personal crises. We want more tangible means. What good is a sign unless we can heal the illness, bring the dead back to life, undo whatever has been done that has gone wrong, or reclaim our lost fortunes and dreams? Why can't God do that for us instead of just giving us signs?

How abandoned we can feel in the crisis times of our lives. When confronted by terminal illness we want the word that a cure is at hand. Why does God allow life to be cut short? In grief and loss we are tempted to blame God, or to question our faith. When relationships fail we are tempted to be bitter and vow to never trust anyone again. At such times we need to tune our ears to hear once again the whisper of God's love.

Of course hearing that whispered message is difficult unless along the way we have cultivated the readiness to listen. That is one of the wonderful things about Christmas; that we can once again tune the receptors of the spirit to the love of

God. It is the message of Christmas that we need to be able to hear in the midst of our tragedies and trials, our struggles and shattered hopes. And if we can claim the gift of God's love in those difficult times, then we really know what Christmas is all about.

Nevertheless it is important for us to remember that Jesus, the sign of God's love, does not banish our problems, but he does illumine them. Christ came into the world to bring light into darkness and hope into despair. He came to restore us to one another and to God. He came to show us the way to reconcile broken relationships and heal a broken spirit. He came to assure us that whatever tempest is about to swallow us up at any moment, we are not alone. Emmanuel! God immanent! God is with us!

Of course we know that in the midst of crisis it is difficult to listen to anything other than what is besieging us. Whether Ahaz and his people would have prevailed against the enemy we do not know. We probably make a mistake in thinking that God intervenes between ourselves and outside forces to protect us. But the intervention of God protects us from ourselves — our faithlessness and our foolishness, and reminds us that we are people of God. Christmas is important because it gives us a brief chance to hear the message clearly once again.

An unusual image suggests itself from another context. Among the time honored traditions of the British armed forces is one rather startling order of discipline. It is rooted in the frank recognition that a cause can be lost in the frenzy of battle when people may begin to act irrationally. At such times people may cease thinking and lose sight of what they should do. So a rule of discipline developed that, at the point where things are at their worst falling apart and all seems in chaos, the commanding officer orders an unmistakable signal whistle to be sounded. And then, whether on a battlefield or aboard ship, as all hell seems to be breaking loose, all activity ceases. The order is that no one is to speak a word or do anything for 30 seconds. During those 30 seconds each person is to say, "I am a British soldier. I am well trained. I will do my best. We shall prevail."

It is a simple concept that we might well employ in our own lives when things become chaotic and out of control. In a sense Christmas gives us such a reminder and a chance to regroup and gain perspective. What does it tell us that we should remember? "I am a child of God. I am loved by God. Jesus has shown me the way to love. And love will prevail."

Have you ever noticed how things eventually quiet down on Christmas Eve? Maybe you are tempted to say, "Yeah, and it is about time!" Our preparation for Christmas is often a hectic experience. We reach the limit of our energy and we become tired and irritable. We're not even ready for Christmas.

Then something wonderful happens. Christmas comes whether we're ready or not. On Christmas Eve, if we allow it, a quietness and expectation steals over us. There is a quiet excitement of the sort that Franz Gruber wrote, and we sing this haunting hymn, "Silent night, holy night ..." For Christ is born among us once again. Christmas Eve's expectation becomes Christmas Day's fulfillment, and the whisper of God's love is spoken once again. Those perceptive enough, as shepherds on an ancient hillside, will hear it. A world sick to death with strife and hatred, disease and pollution, is reminded once more of love and hope.

While some cling to their practiced pessimism, the world is indeed a different and better place after these 2000 years because certain ones of whom Luke wrote long ago were tuned to the unmistakable creative word of God, able to bring hope incarnate as the Child of Bethlehem. A countless host of people from then to now have beheld the power of that quiet Word made flesh.

The power can be a very personal reality. If you are discouraged; if you are lonely; if your life has gone wrong and you need help and strength to find a new way, receive this gift that is coming your way — Emmanuel. God immanent. God is with you. When bodily health fails there is still the gift of God's love. In grief or hardship, in poverty or privation, the reminder at this season is that long ago, to people longing for light in their darkness, a child was given. And to us, as the quietness of Christmas Eve leads us to Christmas Day's joyful celebration of the birth of Jesus, listen intently to hear the whisper of God's love for you. A joyous Christmas to you. Amen.

Give Us
A New Name!

What's in a name? Apparently more than we sometimes realize. Our names are important to us. They carry the message of who we are. Parents think carefully of what to name a new child. How is it going to sound when that child grows to adulthood? Will it be dignified? Distinctive? Pleasant? We want names that will not be embarrassing or cause people to make jokes of them. Probably all of us have been amused by someone's unfortunate name; one probably chosen by a parent who failed to think of the long term effect upon the child of the name they had chosen. A few years ago Johnny Cash sang about "A Boy Named Sue," a hilarious parody of the troubles a kid had going through life with a girl's name. Most of us try to be more sensitive than that and choose names that will wear well enough to last a lifetime, and sometimes names that will be reminders of other beloved or notable people. So many of us are named after others who have gone before us. Jesus, for example, or "Yeshua," as it was more likely said, was the name of the ancient prophet whom we call Joshua. It was a proud and significant name, and according to Luke, told to Mary by the angel visitant before the child was conceived.

Names have sometimes been made to carry messages. The eighth-century prophet Isaiah gave his sons names which were

45

extensions of the message that he wanted his nation to hear. He called his elder son "Shearjashub," meaning "a remnant shall return." So everywhere that son's name was pronounced it expressed Isaiah's confidence in the ultimate return of at least a remnant of the Jews to Palestine from their Babylonian exile. The second son he called "Mahershalalhashbaz," which meant "spoil speeds, prey hastens." Whenever that name was spoken it reiterated Isaiah's contention that Syria and Israel would soon be conquered by Assyria. Perhaps such names were not very fair to the children who had to bear them. I can imagine them wincing under the very statement of their names; probably wishing Dad had called them something a bit more ordinary.

And names have sometimes been used to signify some life-changing event in one's life. You remember that Abram and Sarai were re-named by the Lord as Abraham, meaning, "father of many nations," and Sarah, to commemorate the covenant which the Lord established with Abraham, together with the promise that Sarah would bear a son. (Genesis 17:5f, 15-16) In the New Testament, Saul became Paul, significant of his life-changing conversion on the road to Damascus. And Jesus called Simon, the fisherman, "Petros," or Peter, meaning "rock," significant of his strength. But later when Peter showed signs of weakness Jesus reverted to calling him Simon again, the significance of which the disciples could not have failed to note.

In the missionary days of the 19th and early 20th centuries it was not uncommon for converts to Christianity to adopt a new name significant of their new faith. In our own day some notable persons have changed their names significant of their conversion to the faith of Islam. Thus Cassius Clay became Muhammad Ali, and Lew Alcindor became Kareem Abdul Jabbar. With growing consciousness of ethnic heritage many people — those of African extraction in particular — have replaced family names inherited from the time of slavery with names more nearly representing the African heritage they rightly want to honor. We may ask, "What's in a name?" The answer is, "plenty!"

In the reading for today the Isaiah school of prophecy, which writes under the name of the ancient prophet, predicts the year of the Lord's favor in which, among other things, the messianic people "will be called by a new name." What we hear is effusive and joyful poetry celebrating in anticipation a new relationship between Yahweh and his people in the new age in which the glory of God will transform the life and character of the people. In the day of his coming the theretofore dismal fortunes of the people will be reversed, and all nations will witness Zion's vindication. And that day of vindication will be signaled by their receiving a new name. That new name will remind them forever not just who they are but whose they are. "They shall be called the holy people, the redeemed of the Lord; and you shall be called Sought out, and a city not forsaken." (Isaiah 62:12)

A continuation of the reading for today fleshes out the nature of the Lord's vindication of the people. Remember, they are still exiles, but this is what he wants them to envision.

You shall be a crown of beauty in the hand of the Lord,
*   and a royal diadem in the hand of your God.*
You shall no more be termed Forsaken,
*   and your land shall no more be termed Desolate;*
but you shall be called My delight is in her,
*   and your land Married;*
for the Lord delights in you ....
— Isaiah 62:3-5a

Those words Forsaken and Desolate are written as names, you see. What a terrible thing it would be to be called Forsaken. Like those exiles to whom the prophet wrote, who were sure they would never get out of Babylon, there are people among us in the cities and towns of our own wealthy and privileged land who see their own situation as dismal, miserable and hopeless. Thousands of people live in the desolation of run-down neighborhoods, caught in the helplessness of unemployment or employed at such minimal wages as to be captive to hopelessness that their lot will ever change. Imagine,

47

in the midst of that desolation hearing such good news as, "You shall be called by a new name which the mouth of the Lord will give. You shall be a crown of beauty in the hand of the Lord, . . . for the Lord delights in you." (Isaiah 64:4) It might seem too good to be true.

But that good news is central to our faith. Nobody is forsaken, at least by God. So our very faith in God requires of us that the desolation in our land must change. Proclaiming the love of God and relieving the injustice that holds people as captives in their own land is the job of the community of believers — the church. "For Zion's sake I will not keep silent, and for Jerusalem's sake I will not rest," is the way Isaiah put it. It must be the same for us. As long as people live in desolation and count themselves as forsaken the captivity is not ended. So it is our ministry — yours and mine — to take the issues of human dignity and human opportunity and human brotherhood to the election polls, and to the courthouse, and to city hall, and the state capitol, and to the Congress, and to the White House, until the liberty we so blithely proclaim in patriotic words is a reality in our communities. And if that sounds a bit political to some people, it is. In fact we should be bold to say that it is a distortion of the Christian faith to think that our religious convictions do not have a corresponding action in the world. So it is a spiritual task to which we are called to work and lobby to obtain better housing and equal opportunity to jobs and education and health care and the like because those things are ancillary to our conviction that all people are indeed children of a loving God. Let us be clear that the thrust of our faith is not to gain passage to another world, but to live as the people of God in the present. Therefore our faith work is in this life, and in this world, for this is where people are promised a new name. This is where we proclaim the love of God and the unity of the family of God. Practicing our faith means to declare it and act it out over and over again that we are all children of God, and that we are brothers and sisters to each other. That must be for us the believed and accepted norm for all our human interaction.

Of course some may say that rescuing people from the abyss of poverty and destitution is a cause that can never be won, perhaps even quoting Jesus that the poor will always be with us. But let none deny that there are victories along the way. After all, not all those to whom the hopeful words of Isaiah were addressed realized the hope of release from exile, but some did. Not all the exiles returned to Jerusalem, but a few did. Not everybody heard the angel song at the coming of Jesus, but a few shepherds did. Few even saw a star, but a handful did and followed. Not all of those who feel forsaken and desolate will hear the hope offered them in the name of Christ today, but some will. And thank goodness there are always some hopeful people ready to seize upon the promises of God.

Luke's gospel tells us a hauntingly beautiful story. Jesus' parents dutifully followed the provisions of the law of Moses, and when he was circumcised at eight days they gave him the name Jesus, just as the angel visitant had told Mary before he was conceived. Mary and Joseph took their infant son to the temple to "offer him to the Lord" and to make the customary sacrifice. But there was someone there at the time who opened their eyes to a much greater portent in all this than they had expected. He was an old priest named Simeon; a good and righteous man upon whom, Luke tells us, "rested the Holy Spirit." Simon was one of those hopeful ones, confident in God, and "looking for the consolation of Israel," and who believed that he would not die before he saw the Lord's Christ — the Messiah foretold long ago. Simeon was certainly among a minority of the people with such an expectation or hope, but it burned brightly in him. Imagine the parents' surprise when this incense-drenched old man took the child in his arms and spoke such exalted and prophetic words about him.

> *"Lord, now let your servant depart in peace, according to your word; for my eyes have seen your salvation which you have prepared in the presence of all people; a light for revelation to the Gentiles, and for the glory of your people Israel."*
> — Luke 2:29-32

As though that were not enough, an old woman named Anna, regarded as a prophetess, and who lived in the Temple and spent her time in worship and fasting and prayer, came in at that very hour and began to speak of this child to all who looked for redemption in Jerusalem.

Probably not many took notice of all this. But those two old people were satisfied that they had a sign from God in the person of a little child, whose very name — Jesus — would come to be spoken as the essence of the love of God to humankind. It didn't break like a thunderclap upon those who heard. Even those amazed parents, Joseph and Mary, went home puzzled. Nor years later as he began his ministry did people regard him as at all unusual. "Isn't this the carpenter's son?" they questioned, unaccustomed to the power and authority of his words. Could the message of the truth that makes one free be true for a people existing under the oppressive rule of Rome? Could the assurance of God's love be true for those who languished in poverty? Could the invitation "come unto me" be true for the forsaken, the disheartened, the desolate?

What Isaiah promised to the disheartened exiles Jesus offered to people living in the exile of forsakenness or the desolation of sinfulness and guilt. He offers it still. To people captive to personal problems or addictions, or guilt, or a host of other things he offers a relationship with God to redeem and transform life. It is this good news we tell. It is this new life we are called to live. And it is by a new name that we seek to know others and by which we call ourselves, children of God.

You *Can* Go Home Again!

In 1939, just as the world was teetering on the brink of a war, a world fair was being held in New York. In a sense it tried to push away for a time the threat of impending conflict with lightness and brightness and visions of a beautiful world to come. Nations from all over the world came — the large ones and the small ones. The tiny eastern European nation of Lithuania had an impressive pavillion at the fair where one could see the typical life and culture of that beautiful country. Americans of Lithuanian descent wore their native costumes and did typical national dances. During the fair a production team was making a motion picture to be taken back and shown in movie houses in Lithuania, but their film was never completed or shown, because before the fair closed Hitler and Stalin had divided that little country between Germany and Russia and it ceased to exist.

On March 23, 1992, after 311 days in space, Sergei Krikalev set foot on earth again and found a few changes. The country from which he blasted off did not exist any more. The red hammer and sickle flag emblazoned on his space vehicle no longer denoted a viable political entity. The space agency that sent him aloft was broken up, and even his home town had a new name. Because of the political changes and disputes among newly independent states, what should have been a routine

51

three-month stay aboard the Soviet space station "Mir" lengthened to almost a year, and poor Sergei was stuck up there all that time.

Some people say that you can never return home. Sergei Krikalev might agree. Much of what he left ceased to exist while he was gone. Sometimes we wish we could return home — home to some idealized place and time kept sacred in our memory. Sometimes we try and are disappointed.

Have you ever tried going back just to see some place where you used to live? The neighborhood looks different. The trees are bigger. Strangers who live in the house now look at you with some suspicion as you drive by very slowly, perhaps thinking you're casing the joint. The scene looks familiar in a strange sort of way; your house usually looks smaller than you remember it, and not as warm and friendly. In fact, there is often a nostalgic sadness at being unable to capture what once was but never will be again — even a moment of that time, or a voice, or a loved one. To remain suspended in time, or to return to a former age, must remain the stuff of fiction, not real life. At best we can only look back and recall. We can build upon those events and experiences, and enjoy them, but we cannot alter them.

A man came to my church study one day and, after a brief introduction, got out his checkbook. While I thought that was a good sign, I was not prepared for what came next. "How much for a pair of candlesticks?" he said. That oblique statement was the opening to a story of what had happened seven or eight years before. You see this church had maintained a chapel — which for years had been its principal place of worship before a new larger building was built. That beautiful chapel was open to the public 24 hours a day. There was not even a lock on the door. If that seems incredible, you also need to know that the church was in Los Angeles, California. For 20 years it had never been locked. There had been some occasional minor vandalism, but it remained unlocked. The people wanted it that way.

Then one day an angry young man came to the church and stole the candlesticks and a few other small things. They were worthless to him, but it was done in anger. Things had gone badly for him. Among other things his marriage had failed and he had lost his job. He had gone to a church — not even that one — and felt it was of no help to him. So the theft was to get even. The effect was largely lost because the people at the church didn't know what had happened to the candlesticks. They were not especially expensive ones. So they simply got new ones and went on. And no, they did not put a lock on the door until seven or eight years later.

In the intervening years the guilt over what he had done continued to eat away at this man. Now he found himself in much better circumstances, and looking back realized the stupidity of what he had done. He wanted to make amends and wanted to be forgiven, and while the check was not necessary from our point of view, it was from his. He wrote a generous one. The transaction completed he asked me if I would pray with him, which I did. Then he left my study and I watched as a tearfully happy man walked — almost skipped — out to his car and drove away. I never saw him again. Whatever happened to those candlesticks is far less important than what happened to the man.

Jeremiah spoke in the name of God to a willful and faithless people, saying:

> *"I will not look on you in anger, for I am merciful. . . .*
> *Only acknowledge your guilt, that you rebelled against*
> *the Lord your God . . . and that you have not obeyed*
> *my voice. . . . Return, O faithless children . . . and I will*
> *bring you to Zion."*
> — Jeremiah 3:12b-14, in part

Jeremiah calls for faithless Israel to return, with the promise of leading her to Zion — meaning the habitation of the Lord. There is no promise that the past will be wiped away. In life there is no chance for re-takes. The promise is that the Lord is merciful and "will not be angry forever." In other words, there is the promise of reconciliation.

Each Christmas season for the past several years a television film called *The Gathering*, has aired. It is truly a classic tale with Edward Asner in the role of a man who realizes almost too late his need for reconciliation to the family he loves, but nearly all of whom he has alienated by his hypercritical, arbitrary and beligerant manner. When he discovers he has only a few months to live, he and his estranged wife arrange a family reunion, to which some of the children come gladly and others come only reluctantly. The story is that, in the family celebration of Christmas, the father makes his peace one by one with each of his children. He is not only able to find reconciliation with them, and to love and appreciate them for what they are, but to allow them to return from their own guarded stance of rebellion and its accompanying guilt. Asner's character was able to come home, not to the situation as it had been, but to one he chose to see with new eyes. "I will not look on you in anger," says the Lord, "for I am merciful. Only acknowledge your guilt, that you rebelled against the Lord your God."

Ah, that's the hard part! Admission of guilt! In recent years we have learned a great deal about denial. The alcoholic denies he has a problem with alcohol. The cancer patient denies the illness. In much the same way we deny our own complicity in the situations that alienate us from one another and from God. Moving past the stage of denial is necessary before coming to a healthy acceptance of one's own part so as to get on with life. You can come home again. The wayward son in one of Jesus' stories found that out. But one must come to the admission of one's guilt in at least contributing to the problem in the first place. The admission and acceptance of one's own responsibility for the way things are is so much more difficult than it is to assign the blame to someone else, but Jeremiah tells us it is a necessary step. It is the turning point to life in a new direction.

Jeremiah adds an important idea to the necessity to accept one's own guilt, and that is "I will not be angry with you forever." No one wants to come back to constant recrimination. A runaway child will not come back to constant reminders of guilt and lingering mistrust. A wayward spouse will not return to being constantly reminded of faithlessness. And yet that often happens. "I'll make him come crawling back!" If those are the conditions of coming back, he won't. "I'll never trust him (or her) again!" Who can live with that? No, Jeremiah tells us God deals with us differently. "I will not be angry with you forever," he says. Indeed, if we invite one who is alienated from us to return home, there must be an end to our anger and mistrust, or it won't work. You can return home, but on your part it has to be with new eyes — the eyes of acceptance of one's own part in the problem. It also must be with forgiveness on all parts and the willingness to move forward into a new relationship. Nothing will erase the past. The only answer is to cover it with love.

A priest in Los Angeles has worked for years with runaway young people who, for reasons of their own, are unable to live at home. Some wanted an unrealistic situation of no parental restraints. Others actually suffered under unreasonable limitations and even abuse. But they came face to face with the harsh reality of trying to make it on their own, and like the prodigal son in Jesus' story, and with the help of this street priest whom they came to trust, some were willing to risk an attempt at reconciliation with parents. Oft'times attempts at reconciliation do not work. The same old reactions take over and the situation blows up again. But in a surprising number of cases a counselor is able to work with both parties and help them to build skills for getting along and being sensitive to one another's needs. When several of these reconciliations are ready to take place, they are celebrated with a brief service, ending with the Lord's Prayer. It is a time of high emotion and anxiety, wondering if it is going to work and hoping and praying that it will. As the final prayer is prayed, standing in a circle, all are holding hands. By the time they pray "forgive us our sins, as we forgive those who sin against us,'' people are usually finding it difficult to speak, and before the prayer ends tearful parents and teens are in each other's arms, vowing that the prayer will be fulfilled. ''Return . . . I will not look on you in anger . . . I am merciful . . . and I will bring you to 'the habitation of the Lord.' '' Yes, it is possible to return home.

Alienation is a time of darkness in which we long for light. There was a man named John, who was sent by God to be a witness to the light who was coming into the world. The light, of course, was Jesus. The light was reconciliation and forgiveness and love to cure the darkness of bitterness and alienation and mistrust. To those who decided to accept the gift he gave the power to live as children of God.

We cannot re-live the past. Even if we could we wouldn't do it any more perfectly than we did the first time. We'd just make a different set of mistakes. What we are offered in the name of God is better than that. We can come home forgiven. We can return to where we are loved. We can shoulder our share of the blame for whatever is past and then let it go. Let it drift away and eventually sink out of sight. And we can choose to live as children of God — children of the light. That doesn't guarantee there won't be other times of peril and even darkness. But the promise is that the darkness will never swallow us, and life can go on.

John's gospel gives us that wonderful assurance at the very beginning of the book as he speaks of the coming of the Word into the world in Christ.

> *"What has come into being in him was life, and life was the light of all people. The light shines in the darkness, and the darkness [shall not] overcome it."*
> — John 1:3b-5

That assurance is to every one of us when Christ comes into our lives.

56

Remember
Who(se) You Are

Water!

Water is the most distinguishing characteristic of our planet from the others in our solar system and, from all we know to date, from any other heavenly body in all creation. Water covers most of the earth, and is the reason that, from a vantage point in space, it has a distinctly blue color. Most school children know that now, thanks to a very popular NASA photograph taken from space of this beautiful blue planet with shining oceans, swirling clouds and gleaming polar ice.

The ancient creation theorists had little idea of either the vastness or roundness of the earth, or of the extent to which it is a watery world. Nevertheless, they reasoned that the world originated from and was founded upon a watery abyss, which in some translations of this passage is called "the deep." Their story is that the word of God brings forth creation from primordial chaos. God speaks and it happens. Creation by the Word of God expresses the idea of the absolute sovereignty of God in bringing something out of nothing. Thus, at God's Word light bursts forth and is separated from the night, which is regarded as a remnant of uncreated darkness. So the story goes on that creation proceeds at the Word of a creative God. Not a scientific theory, but a powerful statement of faith. Indeed, powerful events are still put in motion by the Word.

It is important for us to pause a moment and understand what is meant by the (capital letter W) Word of God, as distinguished from a word, or words. By Word we are to understand the very self-expression of God rather than mere words of communication. Thus the scriptures are often referred to as the Word, as we understand God is continually expressed anew through them. So creation took place by the Word or creative expression of God.

Probably few of us regard our own baptism as one of those powerful and creative events, but perhaps it has more potential than we are inclined to believe.

In the springtime, when the winter snows are still melting in the High Sierras, the Yosemite Valley of California echoes with the thunder of waterfalls. Streams and rivers come together in torrents of rushing water, rushing over sheer rock walls in a display of power and beauty. On one such spring day my wife and I approached the base of mighty Yosemite Falls, or at least as close to the base as visitors are allowed to come. Even there one is drenched with the wind and spray from that river gushing over a sheer cliff to crash onto the rocks below. But there was one young man, in his early 20s, who had gone beyond the viewing area to a rock platform off to the side and closer to the falls, where for safety's sake the park rangers would rather people not go. For a long time this young man sat on that rock platform, being buffeted and splashed by the cold spray and wind. He stood up, attempting to shield his eyes from the spray, and tried to look up at the water coming down. Then he raised his arms up in a gesture that seemed to be one of celebration and joy. When at last he had enough drenching he picked his way back over the wet rocks to the pathway. His soaked clothes clung to him, dripping, and his water-filled shoes made a squishing sound with every step. His face was red and numb with cold, but he was laughing and exuberant. "God, I can't believe it." He was almost shouting over the roar of the water, but to no one in particular. "God, what an experience! I'll never forget this as long as I live! I've never felt like this before. Oh, God! It's so awesome!"

His frequent mention of God seemed to be more an expression of emotion and exhilaration than anything religious, but there was clearly some theological implication to what had happened. He went on down the trail waving and smiling at the people who were coming toward him, looking rather surprised as he sloshed by them leaving a trail of water behind. It had clearly been an experience more deeply moving and unique than for most of the people who would probably look a couple of minutes and maybe snap a picture or so and then move on. From his excitement it is likely he would never forget that day. Undoubtedly he would tell of it many times to others who would listen. And one might even surmise that in years to come he will tell it all again to yet undreamed-of children and maybe even grandchildren.[1]

Was your baptism like that? Will you tell of it in glowing terms to anyone willing to listen, or to children or grandchildren? Not likely. Most of us don't even remember our baptism because for us it took place when we were infants or little children. But we know we were baptized. Words were spoken and promises were made; prayers were uttered and water poured, and we were baptized. Baptism, like marriage, is not just done. Rather the sacrament that is begun in churchly rite allows us, if we will, to fill it with meaning as we go along. The indelible mark of the Christ is upon us, ready to remind us of who we are and to whom we belong. It is largely up to us to fill in all the hope and intent that was present at our baptism, and come to realize that we are indeed God's children. God's presence is in us, and upon us the favor of God rests.

On one Sunday morning when there was going to be a baptism, I wanted to help the children present in church that day to understand a little more about what was going on. So at a certain time in the service they came forward. They looked at the baptismal font and the water, and I talked to them about the fact that most of them had been baptized as infants. Water had been placed or poured over their heads and the pastor called them by name and said, ''I baptize you in the name of the Father, Son and Holy Spirit'' and perhaps then also made a special mark — the sign of the cross — on their forehead. The congregation was amused that three or four of the children hearing that reached up and touched their foreheads as though to see if there was anything still there. So we talked about that invisible mark of Christ upon us — a sign of God's love for us, and to remind us whose we are.

Knowing that children like secret messages I had prepared slips of paper, each with a simple message written upon it in lemon juice, so it was invisible. "But, if you take this home and have your mother use a hot iron on it," I said, "the message will appear and you can read it." It is a sign of the passing of time that I forgot that this is a wash and wear generation. On the way home one little girl asked her mother, "Mom, what's an iron?"

The children understood the point, though, that at baptism we are indelibly marked with the reminder that we are children of God. It is not baptism or the symbol of water that makes us children of God. We are all that from the beginning. That is a universal truth of all of us. But in baptism we recognize and affirm that truth with the intent that it will make a difference in us. That is why in baptism parents, and often godparents as well, take upon themselves the obligation to raise these children in the knowledge and love of God and of Jesus Christ, with the intent that when they are older the children will affirm their own faith as believers in God in the way of Jesus.

In the great cathedral of Ghent, in Belgium, there is a wonderful old baptismal font in the shape of a giant globe. The globe is painted bright blue, like our blue planet, and decorated with stars. The globe is surrounded by a great serpent as a reminder that there are less than godly influences loose in the world. At the top of the globe is a cross, to remind us that it is still God's world, but in the world we constantly have to choose between good and evil.

When a child is to be baptized, this globe is hoisted apart by a large chain above the font, and the child is held inside the world. By baptism we do not escape the world. We are simply given the means and power to live in it with the assurance that we are beloved by God, with God's favor upon us. Favor not in terms of privilege, but of the recognition of the opportunity of the power of God to flow through us to change the world. As in the creation story from Genesis we become the new creation by the power and word of God. And the knowledge of who and whose we are in large measure determines our choices in the world.

A fellow pastor had three teenage daughters. They were normal, wonderful, bright, exuberant young people, living life to the fullest. I remember being present one evening when they were going out to a party at the home of one of their friends. They said their good-byes to me and to their parents and headed for the door, which their father held open for them. As they went by he said, "Have a great time, and remember whose you are." It was not said in any heavy or particularly cautionary sense. In fact it was said rather cheerily and lightly, but with just the reminder that there are always choices to make, and those choices are conditioned by who and whose we think we are.

Mark began his gospel with the baptism of Jesus. John the Baptist was preaching and calling people to repentance and baptism in the waters of the River Jordan, symbolic of cleansing and forgiveness of God. He was calling them to new life, and their baptism by water was to be the sign of that turning point in their life. He proclaimed:

> *"The one who is more powerful than I is coming after me; I am not worthy to stoop down and untie the thong of his sandals. I have baptized you with water; but he will baptize you with the Holy Spirit."*
> — Mark 1:8

The inference is that the baptism with water is the beginning. There will be something more to fill and complete it.

Then came Jesus of Nazareth to be baptized. It was clearly a choice Jesus made to define the role he had chosen in answer to the call of God in his life. And here Mark gives us a vision as though through Jesus' eyes.

> *Just as he was coming up out of the water, he saw the heavens torn apart and the Spirit descending like a dove on him. And a voice came from heaven, "You are my Son, the Beloved; with you I am well pleased." (Or "upon you my favor rests.")*
> — Mark 1:10-11

Behold what the Word of God has created this time!

Theologians have differed as to why Jesus came to John to be baptized. Yet by doing so he invites each one of us to our own fulfillment of the baptismal covenant, and to live as people who know we belong to God. He goes before us so we may imitate him and be bearers of the light to all those who suffer in the darkness of adversity or oppression, pain or grief. That's another part of that early creation story; the Word of God once again bringing forth light from darkness. So the fulfilling of our baptism is when the word continues to go forth through us. Imagine that! That means that our part of the baptismal covenant is to live by decision and intent as children of God.

There are so many who live on an accidental basis, and very often with disappointing results. We all need some principle around which to organize our lives so as not to live in selfish or uncreative ways. Certainly there are other reasonable principles around which good and fruitful lives may revolve, for we all know good people who are not the least religious, at least not in any traditional sense. But we have been initiated by our baptism into the way of Jesus as a means of putting us in accord with the Source and Creator of life; the Speaker of the Word. We come to this church today because we continue to make that choice. We do not leave the direction of our lives to chance, nor to someone else's choice, but choose to walk in the way Jesus leads us.

That young man washed by the spray of mighty Yosemite Falls was overwhelmed and inspired by the power of that natural wonder. "God, what an experience," he said. "I'll never forget this as long as I live." So may it be with us who are washed and renewed and changed by the power of God in our lives!

[1]From a sermon by Frederick C. Edwards, published by Liturgical Publications, Inc. Excerpt from *Good News* © published by Liturgical Publications, Inc., 2875 S. James Drive, New Berlin, WI 53151.

Call
Waiting

Samuel was one of those children born rather late in the life of a woman who dearly wanted a child. To have a child was Hannah's most earnest prayer. Indeed the writers of the scriptures regarded a child born late in life as an indication of God's special favor. Hannah, Samuel's mother, must have thought so too, and while he was still an infant, as soon as he was weaned, he was offered into the service of the Lord in thanks to God for his birth. That's how it happened that this young boy named Samuel came to live with and serve as a kind of apprentice under a priest named Eli. Samuel lived and slept right there in what was called the Tent of Meeting, which served as a center of worship years before a permanent temple was built. So he grew up there under the influence of the old priest who was his mentor and example.

The account tells us that Samuel was called by the Lord while Samuel was still a young boy. We don't know how old he might have been. Traditionally the Jews have held that it was probably about age 12, as that was often assumed to be a prime age for spiritual awakening. It happened early one morning, for the scripture tells us that the lamp that burned in the tent all night had not yet gone out. Young Samuel heard his name called — "Samuel, Samuel." Thinking that Eli had called, the boy obediently ran to him, saying "Here I am."

65

But Eli declared he had not called, and told him to go back to bed again. That sounds like an experience most parents have had from time to time with young children. Once again Samuel heard himself called and once again he ran to Eli, but Eli had not called. That kind of thing can get exasperating after a while. And yet a third time it happened. This time it dawned upon old Eli what was happening. He perceived that the Lord was calling young Samuel, so he instructed the boy how to respond.

Now the scripture gives us the idea of a more substantial presence rather than some mere disembodied voice. It tells us "the Lord came and stood there, calling as before, 'Samuel! Samuel!' " This time Samuel answered just as Eli had instructed him and said, "Speak, for your servant is listening." Having gotten his attention, the Lord revealed some surprising things about his future. Thus Samuel was called to his prophetic role. That scene of the drama closes as we are told that when he grew up "the Lord was with him and let none of his words fall to the ground. And all Israel from Dan to Beersheba knew that Samuel was a trustworthy prophet of the Lord." (1 Samuel 3:19-20)

It should be clear to us that Samuel did not come to that calling on his own. He had to be keenly aware of the momentous hopes toward which his parents had projected him in giving him to serve the Lord. And he was under the constant influence of Eli, so Samuel could not help but know about God. Nevertheless there is considerable difference between knowing about and knowing. Knowing about God is secondary based on someone else's knowledge or experience, whereas knowing God is primary, and bespeaks one's first-hand knowledge, experience and relationship. One person's experience shared can become the preparation for another's direct experience and relationship. That can be the powerful effect of our own faith when we share it with another. We have good reason to surmise that is what happened to old Eli and young Samuel. Eli's influence upon the boy at a very receptive time in his life brought him to a state of "critical mass" — the point at which the impact of God directly upon Samuel would not fade away, but be a continuing force throughout his life. Thus Samuel passed the threshhold from knowing about God, to the personal relationship of knowing, and "all Israel, from Dan to Beersheba knew that Samuel was established as a prophet of the Lord."

Eli's very important part in all this was to bring Samuel to the point of readiness, and then to instruct him in the way to respond to the Lord's call. Thus he helped to complete God's revelatory act to Samuel, for without Samuel's response there would have been no relationship. God may call us, but the call awaits our answer.

The story in the scripture is quick to tell us that Eli was not a perfect example. None of us are. The chief criticism of Eli was that he was unable to control his unruly and contemptuous sons. Still God calls us through the imperfect examples of people like ourselves. (Bible scholars feel the condemnation of Eli may have been a later addition.) We may feel some sympathy with Eli if we are at all aware of our own failings. But still God uses us in amazing ways and with a power that often astounds us.

A mother called me one day to invite me to her son's Eagle Scout ceremony. She said, "I want you to see what you helped produce." Of course I was gratified by her comment. Yes, I remember him always being there with his parents, paying attention in a way that seemed beyond his years. And I remember his bright and incisive questions and comments even as a small boy. But I wasn't aware he was looking at me. I wonder, how might I have behaved any differently or said things any more clearly for his benefit if I had known?

Still another mother — a member of a church I had left a couple years earlier — stopped me at a wedding reception one day and wanted to tell me about her daughter. The daughter had been in my church youth group. This mother told me that her daughter had been arrested — and it was not for the first time — for her part in a protest demonstration against the testing of nuclear weapons. When the daughter had telephoned her mother after the arrest her mother wanted to know how she was, and then wanted to know more about why she was so involved in this protest. The daughter explained a bit and then said, "Fred always used to tell us we have to act upon the things we really believe." I couldn't respond in words right then to what this mother had told me because there was a big lump in my throat and tears in my eyes. All I could do was to hug her. How did I know that a young teenage girl had been listening so intently and making all that part of her own life? You may have some similar example from your own experience. Imperfect persons, such as you and I, are indeed used for God's purposes. Remember that. You never know who's looking. You see, we are all guides for someone else, with powers beyond our knowing.

If you know who Eydie Gorme is, you'll know she is a wonderful singer — what we might call a torch singer. On a television talk show a few years ago, Eydie Gorme told some things about how her career got started. Her inspiration and idol was Judy Garland. So Eydie Gorme studied and tried to copy everything that Judy Garland did — the sound of the voice, the style, the mannerisms. Eydie Gorme's first big break came at the Waldorf Astoria in New York City, where she played to packed houses, and received rave reviews. Her next booking was not so elegant. It was somewhere around Pittsburgh in a not-so-classy nightclub — the kind with beer signs flashing in the windows and a pool table in the back.

If that were not a come-down enough, there was a terrible blizzard on her opening night and most people, who might have been there, stayed home. Her second night the weather was even worse. She was there, but there was no audience. The third night she didn't go either. The owner of the nightclub telephoned her and said, "I pay you to sing, and if you don't sing you don't get paid." It made no difference that nobody else had shown up either. She needed the job, so on the fourth night she bribed a taxi driver to get her there through the snow. Besides her there was just the manager, the guy who worked the lights, and part of the band. Some of the players didn't make it either. When it was time for her to sing, the place was still empty, but the house lights were dimmed, the stage lights came on, she cued the band to play her opening music and she began to sing — to an empty house. She said that she told herself, "If I can sing to a packed house at the Waldorf Astoria, I can sing to an empty house here." Part way through the first song the door opened and in the glow of the lights from outdoors she saw the silhouettes of five people who came in and sat at a table in the middle of the room. So she began to sing to those five people. And again she said to herself that she could sing to these five people as she would sing if this was the largest audience Carnegie Hall ever turned out.

She said she sang that night with a richness and a passion and an energy that was as good or better than she had ever sung in her life — to those five strangers. She finished her set, and the spotlight went off and the house lights came on, and she looked out at those five people who had been her audience. Four of them she didn't recognize, but the one in the middle was Judy Garland, who surely had no idea of the power and influence and inspiration she had been in the life of an aspiring young singer named Eydie Gorme.[1]

Yes, we are images for one another. We are influenced by people who may never know it, and others of whom we have no idea may in turn be patterning their life in some small way upon us. Think of those who become a part of you. Think of those who awakened your ideas, and quickened your spirit and encouraged and inspired you. Perhaps for you, as for me, it was a minister who didn't think it beneath himself to sit on the floor and tell stories to children, of whom I was one. Then there was that old man who was still young enough in spirit to take a lively interest in teenage people — to talk to us and even volunteer to take a car load of us when we needed transportation for some youth event. And there was a high school principal who over the years gave up not just hours but days and weeks of his life to lead a YMCA club and often to talk to us about our concerns and the things that were going on in our lives at that age. Those kinds of images are especially important to us when we are young, but we never get past

69

needing someone to lead us into some new way, or the need to see an image in someone else to inspire us.

Mark's gospel tells us that one day John was standing with a couple of his disciples. He saw Jesus passing by, and told them, "Look, here is the Lamb of God." Probably not at all to John's surprise the two disciples left him and followed Jesus. It was an intentional act on John's part. He pointed them beyond himself to Jesus. And when they inquired of Jesus he invited them, saying, "Come and see." So they spent the rest of the afternoon with Jesus. But the story didn't stop there. Andrew, one of the two to whom John had pointed out Jesus, went home and found his brother, Simon, and took him to Jesus. Then the next day as he was leaving for Galilee, Jesus invited Philip to go with him, and Philip in turn told Nathaniel and invited him. Skeptical as Nathaniel was, saying, "Can anything good come out of Nazareth?" he accepted Philip's challenge to "Come and see." You know the result. They all became part of that band of close friends and disciples of Jesus, who after he was captured and crucified, were led by the Spirit to create the movement that evolved into what we know today as the church. It is amazing what happens when, in the simplest of ways, we direct someone's attention to something or someone who can fulfill their lives. We feel flattered when the attention is upon us, but our job as Christians is to be signposts for others, pointing beyond ourselves to the Christ.

I remember a young man who used to enjoy telling how someone led him to become a part of Christ's church. "It all began by spreading fertilizer," he said. You see, this fellow and his wife moved to a new community to take a teaching job, and became acquainted with a neighbor who, he noticed, often went to his church to help out with whatever project was going on there. This young fellow didn't have much interest in church at the time. But one day his new friend invited him, saying, "We could use some help on a project we have going down at the church. How about coming along?" "Sure," he said, "what are we going to do?" "Spread manure," was the reply. True to his word, this young man went along to help put in and fertilize a large lawn. Through that humble task he met some others, and made new friends who took a personal interest in him. The next Sunday he and his wife were in church. It was not long before they became deeply committed followers of Jesus Christ, and an example looked up to by many others, and all because of being invited to do a humble task, and coming to see that these followers of Jesus shared something they wanted in their lives.

God calls us through one another. God leads us through people who sometimes serve as angels unaware, by simply going about doing ordinary things but with the extraordinary presence of God implicit in what they do. How wonderful that God is not off somewhere ignoring us, but calls us in the common events of every day. That call comes to us in the subtle urgings we glean from things we read or see, in the beauty and wonder of creation. It comes in the simple words and lives of people who point beyond themselves to show us the way to God as John did for his disciples. What a wonderful and awesome concept it is that if we listen God can call us to our own destiny through common people like ourselves, and by that same token can call others through us.

We've all had the experience of being put on hold. Perhaps that is where we have put the call of God in our own lives. Old Eli's advice to his young servant Samuel is good advice for us all, to open the communication lines and listen, and say, "Speak, Lord, for your servant is listening."

---

[1]With appreciation to Rev. Robert Morley who brought this story to my attention.

We Know
Jonah

In the spring and summer of 1992, the world was shocked by reports of atrocities and pictures of concentration camps populated by emaciated captives in the strife-torn lands that had been Yugoslavia. No longer held together by a totalitarian regime, ancient feuds and animosities flared into violence and then full-scale war. Heinous acts were committed by Serbian government forces against people of other ethnic and religious groups, under the euphemistic term, ethnic cleansing. People were uprooted from their homes, their property stolen, and told to leave and were told to never come back. Those who resisted were killed or put into camps, where many starved or died of disease, or were tortured or beaten to death. Husbands and wives who were from different ethnic backgrounds were forcibly separated. A most poignant and disturbing image captured by a television camera showed a young boy with stark terror portrayed on his face, who had to remain with one parent, as the other is forcibly driven away.

Terrible things result from the perpetuation of prejudices and stereotypes, rivalries and hatreds. Imagine, for example, being told that you must divorce your wife or husband — the mother or father of your children — because she or he is of a different ethnic or religious background than you. Unthinkable, you say? Perhaps so, but it has happened many times in human history, and still happens. In fact that is exactly what was going on within the Jewish community in the years following the return to Jerusalem from the Babylonian exile, six centuries before the time of Jesus. A national spasm of exclusivism broke out among the Jews, and an open dislike of other nations and nationalities. The result was the division of communities and even families.

Certainly not all Jews felt that way. It may even have been a decided minority. Nevertheless the attitudes of exclusivity and hatred of non-Jews was widespread enough to provoke some brave anonymous literary prophet to write a wonderful bit of allegorical fiction as a protest. It is a literary gem of a short story which masterfully satirizes many prevalent beliefs and attitudes of the time in the person of a man named Jonah. The story depicts the redemptive God in action, and at the same time underlines the concept of the universality of God. By the time of Jesus, Jonah was widely circulated, and the book was accepted officially as part of Jewish prophetic literature by the Synod of Jamnia in the year 90 of the Common Era. Its prophetic importance is acknowledged by the modern Jewish community in that the entire story of Jonah is read each year as the Haftarah (Prophetic scripture selection) for the afternoon service on Yom Kippur, the Jewish Day of Atonement.

This anonymous author opens the door for us to assume several things about Jonah — that he was a proud man, self-centered, arrogant and opinionated. He was headstrong and willful, and used to getting his own way, by hook or crook, as we might say, regardless of others. Certainly very important among Jonah's characteristics is the fact he harbored some very deep-seated prejudices, especially against certain groups, chief among them the city-state of Nineveh. Ironically, that is the very place the Lord picked out for Jonah to go and preach.

It seems that Jonah also had a quick temper, and a rather strong tendency to vindictiveness. Sounds like just the person you'd like to know, doesn't he? And yet we have to say of

Jonah that he was undoubtedly a good man by commonly held standards. He certainly must have thought of himself as a righteous man. He believed in God, and no doubt he knew the scriptures, obeyed the law, and was regular at prayer. Jonah was typical of many Jews. In fact the author's intent seems to be that many Jews, reading this story, would see themselves in Jonah.

The story is that the word of God came to Jonah to go to Nineveh, and to preach to the people of "that great city," and call them to repentance, but Jonah disliked that prospect and hopped on a ship bound in the opposite direction, to Tarshish. The obvious implication was that not only Jonah, but the Jewish people were disobedient to God. God said to do one thing, and Jonah did the opposite.

The ship Jonah boarded sailed out of Joppa, and another fine irony is that in running away from one despised group of foreigners, Jonah put himself in the hands of another, which has some interesting implications. When a storm came up, Jonah was asleep, while the sailors he would have called pagans were not only trying to keep the ship afloat, but praying to their gods. Thus they proved to be more devout, in their own way, than Jonah. In fact, the captain woke Jonah and demanded that he, too, call upon his God, lest they all perish.

Jonah knew he was the problem, and the solution, he said, was for the sailors to throw him overboard. But these despised pagan sailors proved to be more compassionate and humane than that, and chose instead to row as hard as they could for shore. When at last they had no other choice but to throw him overboard they offered a sacrifice and made vows to the Lord. Thereupon the Lord "appointed a big fish" to swallow Jonah, who spent three days contemplating his situation there in the belly of the fish, and in desperation turned again to the Lord.

When the fish conveniently vomited Jonah up onto the dry land the word of the Lord came to Jonah a second time to go to Nineveh, and proclaim the message that I tell you. Jonah's prayer within the great fish didn't sound all that repentant. Still he arose and went to Nineveh and proclaimed the message of the Lord. According to the story the people of Nineveh "believed God," and "they proclaimed a fast and put on sackcloth," as a sign of repentance, "from the greatest of them to the least of them." Of course that is just part of the story. Some of the best is yet to come, but I leave you to read that last chapter on your own.

Jonah must have been amazed at his success, but he was also angry. You see, Jonah had not wanted to be all that successful. Despite his experience in the fish, and the fact the Lord had given him another chance, he had not changed a whole lot. He still nursed his prejudices, and would have been quite happy to see the Ninevites be destroyed after all. He even built himself a little shelter above the city so he'd have a ring-side seat when that happened. He even had more pity for the vine that grew up over him to shade him, and then was attacked by a worm and died, than he had for the people of that great city of Nineveh.

The strife of Serbs and Croats and Bosnians and Muslims is half a world away from us. The painful road of Black Africans to equality in the Union of South Africa is an occasional article in a newspaper or news magazine. The holocaust of six million Jews and five million other human beings was half a century ago. And this Jonah of the scriptures was probably not even a real person, and certainly the events that are recorded didn't even happen. So we can forget all this, right? Or we can read the story of Jonah and argue about its historicity, or whether a fish could swallow a man, and miss the point! But if we read Jonah with the sense that it has something important to say to us, we might then paraphrase Walt Kelly's "Pogo," and say "We have seen Jonah, and he is us!"

No, we must not be isolated from those strife-torn places in the world. The holocaust is part of our history that if we fail to learn from it humanity may one day repeat. The biblical story of people sometimes following and as often disobeying God is our story, too. The Jews read Jonah on the Day of Atonement as a reminder that it not only spoke to those people of Bible times, but speaks to us today. In a world where people find numerous reasons to divide themselves from one another, we need all the more to proclaim the universality of God, and the commonality of the human family.

The unfortunate tendency is for us to maintain the insular attitude and fiction that exclusivism and prejudice are someone else's problem, not our own. Jonah, in the biblical story, never really confronted the fact of his own prejudice. Perhaps that prophetic author is telling us that neither do we really confront our own racism, our prejudice, our exclusivism, either as a society or as individuals. And while those attitudes may become institutionalized as accepted social practice, and speech, and even law, that only happens with the consent of individuals.

In a program examining the roots of anti-Semitism in Nazi Germany of the 1930s and early '40s, Bill Moyers interviewed Fritz Hippler, who had been in charge of propaganda under Adolph Hitler. In one of his terrible and vicious propaganda films the Jews were compared to rats which spread disease. Of that film and the others he produced he said, ''We didn't know what the effect would be — what was going to happen. We did our job.'' How easily and conveniently one can sidestep responsibility. As Moyers said concerning the people that film was intended to influence, ''Not much imagination was required to think of what to do with the Jews.'' And Hitler readily admitted that the propaganda he produced played upon the anti-Semitism that already existed among people — the ideas and attitudes in the minds of ordinary people.

From the comfortable distance of 2,300 years we may be indifferent about the matter of Ninevites — whoever they were — but scratch below the surface of any of us and almost for certain there is a bit of prejudice there. Most of us try to control it, especially in circles where expressions of prejudice are not socially acceptable, but it is there.

Don't take me wrong, though. We're good people. We know we are. We work hard. We are reasonably honest. We love and are devoted to our families. We support good causes. We stand up for public morality and honesty and treat our neighbors with respect. We want a peaceful world where everyone is fed and housed. We go to church and worship and pray. But in all fairness we should say that all those things probably represented Jonah, too. Yes, Jonah tells us something about ourselves.

Jonah warns us about ourselves and the attitudes we perpetuate. If God is a universal God, whose redemptive love is for all people, then how can we exclude anyone from the circle of our love? And yet in the time of Jesus those exclusive ideas were still around. It was precisely to counter the Jews' hatred of Samaritans that he chose to make a Samaritan the hero of one of his stories, for to the Jew the word neighbor referred only to another Jew. Jesus even had to contend with a couple of his own disciples who were ready to call down fire from heaven to consume the people of an inhospitable Samaritan village. Jesus himself, though, offered water — spirit — that would spring up and never cease, to a Samaritan woman he met at Jacob's well one day, whose life needed to be redeemed from the mess she had made of it. Here was the redemptive action of God personified in Jesus.

Ideas of prejudice and exclusiveness are among the most insidious and sinister of social diseases. They divide person from person, group from group, class from class, race from race, faith from faith, and nation from nation. In the circle of our own friends most of us hear the gay-bashing remarks, and the not-at-all-innocent jokes that disparage and demean other races and nationalities, and by people that we know and like. We know the embarrassment; the awkwardness and pain of trying to separate ourselves from those attitudes without destroying a friendship. Sometimes that is a fragile balance to maintain, and a risk we must take to venture into that hazardous darkness of another's prejudice.

People of good will, and certainly the followers of Jesus, must forthrightly disavow exclusivism, whatever be the excuse. Of course prejudice always is substantiated by reasons, but it cannot be supported by any appeal to the God of compassion and love we have seen revealed in Jesus. On the contrary the people of God are called to proclaim the universality of God and the commonality of all humankind. The darkness of disparagement of other people must be banished by the light of love. We are called to bring light into the darkness, which is what this season of Epiphany is to remind us.

A young Gulf Coast fisherman was one of many who viewed with considerable alarm and anxiety the influx of Vietnamese fishermen into the area. The Vietnamese, of course, were refugees who fled their own country, and after coming here began to engage in the only trade they knew — fishing. But the fishing industry was already beset by foreign competition and low prices, and did not welcome further competition from these new immigrants. Some terrible things were done in a futile attempt to turn back the threat. There were brawls and threats of further violence. Nets were cut, and a couple boats were torched. The situation threatened to get totally out of hand. Some hotheads were even talking of violence against the immigrants' families. This young man found himself in the quandary of wanting to defend his livelihood, but he was shocked and disturbed by the violence. He had never taken part, and stood well clear of the vicious talk and harrassment of the Vietnamese. He remembered that his father had been an immigrant from Portugal and had borne his own share of discrimination in earlier days. This young fisherman and his wife, both devout Catholics, believed that the way of Jesus required something different of them than to hate and despise other people. They talked about it and decided they must do something.

The next evening they went to visit one of the Vietnamese homes nearby, and took their small child with them. The Vietnamese fisherman — a man about his own age — met them at the doorway, at first wary and afraid. After an awkward pause he invited them in. Uncomfortable with one another at first they sat around a kitchen table and began to talk — two young couples learning something of each other and the hopes that each had for themselves and their children for the future.

Bit by bit they learned something of each other and found that though they began a world apart they had much in common. They agreed that whatever the problems that may lie ahead they could face them better together. As the night wore on to the early hours of the morning, they shared some food and drink, a handclasp, and even some genuine laughter. In Oriental tradition a gift was given — a small framed painting of a Buddhist shrine in their home village in Vietnam. Caught by surprise, and thinking they ought to give something in return, the American woman reached into her purse and pulled out a rosary she always carried with her and handed it to the other woman.

It was a small incident certainly, but at least between two families there is a bridge of understanding and respect and the beginning of trust. In a Catholic Christian home a picture on the wall of a Vietnamese Buddhist shrine is a constant reminder of that momentuous beginning, as is a rosary hanging on a wooden peg near the Buddhist shrine in a Vietnamese-American home.

The Jonahs of our time would like to avoid that venture saying, "Oh God, I don't want to do that," or "Don't send me there. Not to those people." So often our prejudices stand in the way of our doing what God calls and prods us to do. Our more probable reaction is to just claim to be too busy, or allow inertia to be the pocket veto against our doing anything. Still as we try to escape it the call of God pursues us, and offers us another chance to go and show forth the very God of forgiveness and reconciliation and compassion that we talk about. And the epiphany of God comes afresh in us whenever the light of God in us pushes back a bit farther the curtain of darkness that forever threatens, and whenever we include another human being in the circle of our love.

A Prophet
Like Me

Most people have a rather warped view of the biblical prophets. We have tended to see them as rather like a man I saw outside Saint Stephen's Cathedral in Vienna, dressed in what looked like bed sheets, wearing a beard, with a sign around his neck, and carrying a staff, and shouting things to anyone who happened to look his way. He reminded me of some of the cartoons I had seen in the *New Yorker* magazine, depicting long-bearded characters in similar dress, usually announcing the end of the world. Certainly some of the prophets had their own peculiarities and sometimes dramatic ways of getting their messages across. If one includes John the Baptist in that prophetic tradition, one must also note some strange tastes in food and dress.

To consider the prophets as mere eccentrics or troublemakers is to diminish their importance, which is exactly what many people tend to do with their modern counterparts. To do so makes them easier to ridicule or ignore. Those who would counter prophetic stands tag them with a catch word such as radical, or extremist, and other good words like liberal and conservative take on a severely pejorative tone.

The prophetic tradition is probably one of the most valuable contributions of Hebrew religion, tracing back to nomadic times when, at Horeb, a fearful people asked for a mediator between themselves and God, and got Moses. For a long time it seemed that Moses would be the only prophet, but in today's scripture we hear a farewell address to the people, who were about to enter Canaan without him. In it Moses prepares the way for other prophets who will follow him, evidently on the assumption the people will continue to need that sometimes encouraging, sometimes prodding mediator between themselves and God:

> *The Lord your God will raise up for you a prophet like me from among your own people; you shall heed such a prophet. This is what you requested of the Lord your God at Horeb . . . .*
>
> — Deuteronomy 18:15

And of this prophet, the Lord says:

> *I will raise up for them a prophet like you from among their own people; I will put my words in the mouth of the prophet, who shall speak to them everything that I command. Anyone who does not heed the words that the prophet shall speak in my name, I myself will hold accountable.*
>
> — Deuteronomy 18:18-19

These are strong words! And thus in the scriptures we do not hear the prophets speak on their own behalf, but with a far greater authority, saying, "Thus says the Lord!" Remember there was as yet no priesthood or holy rite, and no temple, and yet the wandering tribes of Israel had one among them who spoke for God. Even when they became a settled people the prophetic heritage begun in the desert was never forgotten. Of course in time various kings hired their own professional court prophets, who said what the king wanted to hear. That's what they were paid to do. Modern leaders tend to do the same thing. Not many critical voices are heard very near presidents or monarchs or other heads of state. But the great prophets of the scriptures were not professional prophets.

82

Their call to their prophetic task rose out of faith in God and genuine concern for the welfare of the people and the nation.

These were not always popular. Nathan, the prophet, risked his neck when he confronted King David about his affair with Bathsheba and the murder of her husband. King Ahab called the prophet Elijah, "you troubler of Israel," and Jeremiah was confined for a time in the mire at the bottom of a pit because there were some who wanted to silence him. On a couple occasions Jesus referred to the persecution, and even the killing of the prophets. So the people and their leaders became angry with the prophets and stoned and ridiculed them, but could not keep from producing them in every generation. God kept calling forth prophets from among the people, and the Hebrews could not deny that God spoke through them, even though they often did not want to hear them.

Prophet ought to be part of the definition of every Christian. It was Peter who reminded ordinary people, "You are sons of the prophets." (Acts 3:25) I happen to believe what the church has maintained throughout its existence, that God still calls forth those special prophets from our midst. Nevertheless, being prophetic is still not especially popular. Prophetic words and actions are unpopular by the very nature of trying to get the majority to consider the consequences of where the present path will lead. Saying unpopular things is part of the job description, but it should be part of the job description of anyone in Christian ministry. I remember hearing the admonition to some new ordinands to beware of being too well thought of. Of course we want to be well liked, but let none of us be thought harmless or ineffective in proclaiming the Word in prophetic fashion. Even so it is one of the least appreciated aspects of ministry. It opens one to criticism, and hence some lose all but a faint glimmer of prophetic ardor for popularity sake, or even for self-preservation.

Churches tend to silence prophetic preachers. They do it very effectively by withdrawing support, or by trumping up some other excuse to get a pastor moved. Our division of human affairs into the artificial categories of sacred and secular inveighs heavily against prophetic ministry, because it assumes that religion has no right to be a critical and moral corrective in collective human affairs or politics, or in any other than the personal arena of the individual's relationship to God. Yet few raise questions about the religion-laden pious preachments of politicians whose own participation in religion may be tangential at best, but who invoke religious phrases to support partisan political ideas and presume to set the agenda for what the religious institutions ought or ought not to be doing. But the biblical prophetic tradition is that religion must not be the handmaiden of politics, nor merely reflect commonly accepted social patterns, but must be critical of both.

Church denominational bodies are often too diverse and unwieldy, or fearful of the consequences, to be truly prophetic. A few denominations have been prophetic on particular themes, earning great respect, and perhaps even causing others not of their persuasion to at least consider their own beliefs and course of action. The Society of Friends and the Mennonites, for example, plus a few other groups have done a splendid job of consistently taking a forthright stand for peace and against war. They have not forced it upon anyone else, in the true prophetic tradition, but they have caused many others to consider that the war option is too easily chosen in an attempt to resolve international disputes.

Occasionally a major church body does take a bold prophetic stand, knowing full well that there will be consequences to accept. Being prophetic is not a popularity contest. Sometimes being prophetic even means taking the side of someone with whom you profoundly disagree. The United Presbyterian Church made such a move some years ago in contributing a small amount of money to the defense fund of a young black woman college professor. They did not do so because they agreed with her views. They most decidedly did not. They did it because they believed she had been dismissed from her position without due process, which is the right of every citizen under the Constitution of the United States of America, regardless of their views. They did it to be heard and to make

84

a witness about the climate of fear and hatred that was loose in the land. It was to say that in God's name this is not right! But people heard what they wanted to hear. People left Presbyterian churches in droves, and even whole congregations separated themselves from the denomination. The United Presbyterian Church was accused of being communist, and unpatriotic, and untrue to the gospel, and all sorts of things. Unfortunately, the point was lost on many people who were moved more by their own political agenda, and by fear, than by a reasoned sense of the rightness, and the necessity of treating every person justly. The stand was prophetic, but the effect upon the denomination was disastrous. Prophetic stands are often misunderstood, and one remembers poor Jeremiah suffering there where he had been thrown into the mire at the bottom of a pit. His prophecy was not well received either.

Some of the things we assume ought to be understood and accepted by everyone are not, and to proclaim what seems obvious to us turns out to be prophetic. Some years ago the art department of a Roman Catholic college in California was invited by a large multi-national corporation to decorate its New York office building for Christmas. The only requirement was that the finished product reflect the theme of Christmas. So teachers and a few students went to New York to measure the wonderful long window space where thousands of people passed by each day. Back home again they got busy with ideas and drawings, and then they hand-painted hundreds of folding cartons such as are used for moving household goods, and shipped the flattened cartons to New York for assembly in the windows.

When the windows were unveiled and the display appeared, it said simply, "PEACE ON EARTH," in large letters that could be read from wherever that window could be viewed. Walking by closer to the window one could read quotations from several internationally known people on the theme of peace — Pope John XXIII, Martin Luther King, Jr. and Dag Hammarskjold, among them. It was an impressive and attractive display, and the students and their teacher were pleased. Besides, they had given this wealthy corporation a stunning

Christmas window at bargain basement cost. But they were not prepared for what followed. People walking by were disturbed. There were no things to look at in the window. There were no lights and decorations and trees, only this wall of painted boxes proclaiming peace on earth. Letters came to the corporate office from people and nearby businesses wondering what sort of political message might be intended. And a letter came to the college art department from the corporation's head office saying exactly what many people on the streets of New York had been asking, "What does that have to do with Christmas?"

Indeed, what does peace on earth have to do with Christmas? Now 11 weeks after Christmas, our decorations are safely stored away for another year, but the angelic song of peace on earth is a prophetic word of God to a wounded and war-weary world, put into our mouths to proclaim, "I shall put my words into the mouth of the prophet, who shall speak to [the people] everything that I commanded." We are the prophets with a message on our tongue so that the Herod schemes of today will not succeed after all. To proclaim the Word is our prophetic task as the Church of Jesus Christ. As such we do not offer a panacea, but a new mind and a new view.

It is very easy to be critical of the church when it fails to be as prophetic as it should, but let us not forget that we are the church. The church's task of being prophetic is our job. We are the descendants of the prophets, and ours is the inheritance to be prophetic. Sometimes individually we have to assume the prophetic role within and to the church, and always be in touch with human need.

Mark's gospel tells us that at the beginning of his ministry, Jesus entered the synagogue on the sabbath day and began to teach. The people were astounded at his teaching. He taught them as one who had authority. But part of the same story is that after he left the synagogue he went over to the house of his friend Simon, and found that Simon's mother-in-law was in bed with a fever. Mark tells us that "he took her by the hand and lifted her up." That is an important aspect of prophetic ministry that we must always keep in mind. Our prophetic words will be effective only if we keep in mind that we must always uplift people.

Performing the prophetic role must also assume a willingness to understand the Word in the scriptures, and apply its wisdom to contemporary life. The word of God is not something drawn out of the blue. It is put in our mouths as a result of study, and prayer, and reflection, and discussion. Being a prophet is work. To be prophetic one must see the big picture. We must have a sense of history and a grasp of moral law, and the understanding that certain choices bring about predictable results. Most of all the prophet views every act from the awareness that God speaks to contemporary situations and to our own lives.

Implicit in our Christian faith we have the belief — indeed the experience — that God still speaks to humankind. God may not always say what we want to hear, and we must never confuse our own opinions with the will of God. But as individuals, and together as the church, we must cultivate the sensitive ear and the willing heart that we may be reached by God in every situation. Every generation needs those who are raised up as prophets from the midst of the people to speak the Word and to act in the name of God. Perhaps our own generation needs the prophetic voice most of all.

Feeling Down
And Looking Up

The scripture for today is from the portion of Isaiah which scholars know as Deutero-Isaiah, or Second Isaiah — chapters 40 to 55. Those chapters certainly were not written by the eighth century B.C.E. prophet whose name it bears, but rather by an anonymous observer of the events in the closing years of Babylonian rule, and who interpreted the meaning of those events to the Jewish exiles in Babylonia. A momentous event stirred him to prophesy to the captives, and that event was the rise to power of Cyrus, who this prophet saw as the Jews' ticket to freedom. Even more than that, he saw Cyrus as the instrument of God, for he granted the Jews freedom to return to their homeland. However, the people had become dispirited in their captivity and had lost the hope of ever returning. In fact the prevailing mind-set was to accept the inevitable, make the best of their situation, and to remain in Babylonia.

Thus the prophetic task was to rouse the people's hopes and prepare them to take advantage of the freedom, which Cyrus granted them, and to return. The prophet had to arouse in them a renewed faith in God, and to stir in them longings and hope for a homeland. Before the exile there had been stern rebukes and warnings of doom and punishment. Indeed those earlier prophets had seen Jerusalem's defeat and the exile as instruments of God's judgment. But now the purpose of the prophetic word is to turn them toward a future filled with glorious promise, soon to be fulfilled.

He begins with words of comfort, with an older definition meaning to strengthen, rather than to soothe, and then he proceeds to recite the mighty power of God, whose supremacy is over the whole world. Nowhere else in the scriptures is the omnipotence of God proclaimed more eloquently than in these words:

> *Get you up to a mountain, O Zion, herald of good tidings;*
> *Lift up your voice with strength, O Jerusalem, herald of good tidings,*
> *Lift it up, do not fear;*
> *Say to the cities of Judah, "Here is your God!"*
> *See, the Lord God comes with might, and his arm rules for him;*
> *His reward is with him, and his recompense before him.*
> *He will feed the flock like a shepherd;*
> *He will gather the lambs in his arms, and carry them in his bosom,*
> *And gently lead the mother sheep.*
> — Isaiah 40:9-11

And then to the portion for today:

> *Have you not known? Have you not heard?*
> *Has it not been told you from the beginning?*
> *Have you not understood from the foundations of the earth?*
> *It is he who sits above the circle of the earth,*
> *and its inhabitants are like grasshoppers;*
> *who stretches out the heavens like a curtain,*
> *and spreads them like a tent to live in;*
> *who brings princes to naught,*
> *and who makes the rulers of the earth as nothing.*
> — Isaiah 40:21-23

Sometimes even the best of opportunities appear more as problems. The Jews' experience in captivity led them to conclusions other than what these eloquent prophetic phrases were telling them. They were convinced that Yahweh had failed to help them, and even that their God had been defeated by the gods of Babylon. They were downhearted and inwardly, at least, still a defeated and dejected people.

Still this Second Isaiah would not give up. He had learned a few things during those years of captivity. Some revelations had come his way that had not been known in Palestine before the exile, for he and the other captives had come to the greatest center of culture and knowledge in the whole world. While the familiar Jewish writings spoke of the creation of God, and the psalmists extolled the moon and stars as God's handiwork, they knew relatively little about the heavens. But here in Babylonia, astronomy was quickly becoming a science, and it opened the mind of the prophet to wonders beyond his imagination. So now he met the people's downcast visage with a triumphant and informed faith. To those who are feeling down he said, "Look up!"

> Lift up your eyes on high and see: Who created these?
> He who brings out their host and numbers them,
>   calling them all by name; because he is great in strength,
>   mighty in power, not one is missing.
> What do you say, O Jacob, and speak, O Israel,
>   "My way is hidden from the Lord, and my right is
>   disregarded by my God?"
> Have you not known? Have you not heard?
> The Lord is the everlasting God,
>   the Creator of the ends of the earth.
> He does not faint or grow weary;
>   his understanding is unsearchable.
> He gives power to the faint, and strengthens the powerless.
> Even youths will faint and be weary,
>   and the young will fall exhausted;
> but those who wait for the Lord shall renew their strength,
>   they shall mount up with wings like eagles,
>   they shall run and not be weary,
>   they shall walk and not faint.
>
> — Isaiah 40:25-31

Deutero-Isaiah's ebullient message is to downcast people of every age. Literally thousands in our midst are captive to hopelessness and misery. Their experience, like the exiles, leads them to believe something other than the hopeful message of the prophet.

On December 24th, nearly 20 years ago, a lovely young woman in her mid-20s appeared at the church in the morning and wanted to talk. I had the feeling it might take a while, and considered the fact that in the evening there was going to be a festive Christmas Eve service, and my part of the preparation was not nearly done. After expressing my dilemma aloud she suggested she would enjoy helping, and we could talk as we worked. So we talked and worked, and went out and talked through lunch, and talked and worked some more on into the afternoon. As it turned out I had known her as a little girl and had known her parents. She came from a fine family.

She was young and beautiful, and intelligent, and well educated, and articulate, and it would seem she had everything going for her. Yet she struggled with seasons of depression, and in between those she never really felt good about herself. In her late teens she had ceased having any participation in the church. But later on, thinking that religion might be the answer to some of her problems, she linked up with a small religious group. It was not much like the church in which she had grown up, and it didn't help matters at all. They placed a lot of emphasis on sin and salvation, and she never seemed to be able to get beyond the sin part. She was convinced she was a sinful person and needed to be saved and born again, but she was unable to feel the forgiveness of God, or any release from the guilt that oppressed her.

I told her about the God of love I believe in, ready to forgive us if we will but accept it, and that we must also forgive ourselves. We talked of the things she hoped and dreamed of in her future, and the person she wanted to be. I reminded her of all the people who loved her.

We talked and worked together most of the day. At one point, she said, "You're really a very happy person aren't

92

you?'' I acknowledged that at least most of the time I am. ''I wish I could be like you,'' she said. ''And I hope I can feel that God loves me. I don't feel that right now.'' ''I believe you can,'' I assured her, ''and I'll do my best to help you.''

By the end of the day I was exhausted — not from the physical work I had been doing — that was easy — but from the emotional strain of trying to lift the spirits of this young woman and help her look up and see an abundant life awaiting her. Before she left she said, ''This has been a good day. In fact this has been the happiest day I can remember.'' She was smiling. Her speech was animated. ''And you might even see me in church tonight,'' she said. We prayed together, and she hugged me and promised to come back to talk again right after Christmas, and then she went away.

I looked for her in church that night. She was not there. I looked for her again on Sunday morning, but she was not there. I never saw her again. I had no way to get in touch with her. Two weeks after our conversation I learned that she died alone beside a lonely road. She had taken her own life.

I could hardly get her out of my mind for the next several weeks. I think of her now nearly 18 years later, and I have an empty feeling where a pleasant memory of her should be. I have often wondered what I could have done or said that would have made the difference, and how I wish I had another chance to try. My only consolation is that I helped her have one fine day of joy and hope.

One does not overcome a deep-seated and long-term feeling of despair in a few hours, or even in a few days. That is why anyone suffering from depression or that inward-spiraling feeling of worthlessness, or even lesser problems of self-image, should immediately seek quality counseling and stay with it on a consistent basis long enough to do some good. That young woman was not even able to believe in herself, much less could she believe in and trust the God-presence with her, or within her, to forgive and affirm her.

It is sad but true that many of the people who are captive to feelings of hopelessness are young people. ''My way is hidden from the Lord, and my right is disregarded by my God.'' That's a way of saying, ''Nobody knows and nobody cares about me, least of all God,'' and many would add, ''If there is a God.'' A surprising number of young people, with what should be the best of life ahead of them, are often so despondent that they commit suicide. Suicide among teens is increasing at an alarming rate. Hospitals and teen counseling centers broadcast telephone numbers on television and radio hoping that some of these, or their families or friends, will call. If you know such a disturbed young person, perhaps the most caring thing you can do is to put them in touch with such a place. There is no stigma attached to seeking help. In fact, rather than a sign of weakness, it shows strength and courage. This is a message that we must communicate to the down-hearted and discouraged and despondent, to look up and see the evidences of the loving and redeeming God. Of course one of the best ways is to show them that loving, caring and accepting presence in ourselves.

At the counter of a coffee shop where I used to go rather frequently, I sat beside a man I had seen there several times before. He was always alone. So this time I decided it might be good to get acquainted. We learned each other's names. His was Paul. After a little conversation we found we enjoyed each other's company, and over the next three years until I moved, we met often and sat together in one of the booths to talk.

Paul was a quiet sort of man, and not given to talking much about himself, so it was several months before he told me he had been in prison. He hadn't told me up to that time because he was afraid of rejection. It had happened many times before. I considered it an indication of great trust that he told me at all. ''I've done some terrible things,'' he told me, ''but, no, it wasn't murder.'' He was nearly 70 when I knew him, and he had been out of prison for nearly 20 years, but up to the time he was 50 he had spent more than half his life behind bars. Now he was free, or at least his body was free. He could come and go as he chose. And possibly because he had spent so many years locked up, he would often ride for miles in the open country on his motorcycle. But Paul, like those to whom the message of Deutero-Isaiah was addressed, was still a prisoner of sorts. He was sure nobody would want to know him if they really knew about his past. He was afraid nobody would trust him, even though he had been a law-abiding citizen for years. He was haunted by his past — that part of his life he had wasted, and that had colored so much what he thought of himself.

I found out something else about Paul, though. He lived in a tiny house in a rather run-down area of the town inhabited mostly by older folks living on small pensions. Paul spent most of his time working for those people and doing whatever needed to be done — fixing a roof, repairing a faucet, digging a garden, or building a fence. He didn't charge anything except for materials. He knew those people needed help with things they were unable to do for themselves. He said, "I guess this is a way I can make up a little bit for what I did earlier on in life. I'm really happy, and can forget the past for a while, when I'm doing something for somebody else." Part of Paul will always be the captive. Another part of him is still struggling and learning to be free. I like to think that what was shared in our friendship helped free him a bit more.

Now someone may say that doesn't sound like much of a success story. Of course we like to hear those stories of how someone's life is changed dramatically, and those happen occasionally. Most often our successes are small ones. You know it is strange the way we measure success. A baseball player with a batting average of .330 is a good hitter. However, if that is good we need to keep in mind that two of every three times he comes up to bat, he fails! That might even have been about what that ancient prophet's average was, too. Despite his best efforts probably most of the exiles or their descendants stayed where they were — in Babylonia. We must never be discouraged for lack of dramatic success. Perhaps there is more impact on the lives we touch than is apparent.

Jesus had an amazing power to uplift people, in ways more than just the curing of bodies. I think that is why, when he healed someone, he was as likely to say "your sins are forgiven," as to say "rise up and walk." Jesus had the ability to free people from whatever power, real or imagined, kept them from living full and fulfilled lives. I am convinced we have that same healing quality. In fact Jesus himself indicated to his disciples that they would do even greater things than they had seen him do.

You and I encounter people every day who are downcast and have forgotten, if they ever knew, how to look up and behold the presence of God. They need to be strengthened (comforted) and lifted up. We may get only one chance. We may not always be remarkably successful. But the good news is that no situation and no person is hopeless, and that God can move through us with power and grace to redeem and renew life. To those who are weary of all hope we declare the God who "does not faint or grow weary." To those who are sure nobody understands, we proclaim the God whose "understanding is unsearchable." To those faint-hearted and afraid to try, we promise "the Lord shall renew their strength. They shall mount up with wings like eagles. They shall run and not be weary. They shall walk and not faint." Like Jesus we must embody those qualities of hope, and understanding, and acceptance, and love, and encouragement, and compassion just as Jesus did. And if anyone should ask us beyond that how we can be so certain that God is in charge of creation and cares for them, invite them out on a clear starry night and say to them some of the things that ancient prophet said to his dispirited people. "Look up. Who created these, and called them by name? Then how could any of us be absent from God's care and love?"

Epiphany 6
2 Kings 5:1-14

Wade In
The Water

The lives of the rich and famous hold a strange fascination for those of us who do not find ourselves in that category. From a very surface view it is easy to envy their glamorous and opulent lifestyles. How we'd like to be like them. We could really enjoy having their money, or their influence, or the adulation of the people who crowd around them. How nice it would be to have the athletic prowess of Michael Jordan, or the good looks and acting talent of a Tom Cruise or Geena Davis, the voice of Luciano Pavarotti or Natalie Cole. Is there any one of us who would not like to be cast in the limelight of fame and fortune, at least for a while? And living in a posh house with the choice of a luxury car or so and a sports car wouldn't be bad either, or meeting other famous people, or taking vacations in exotic places around the world. Sounds great, doesn't it? Anyone want to sign up?

Of course I forgot to tell you that you have to sign up for the whole package, not just for the good stuff. Those are the rules. I told you this was just a surface view, from which we mostly tend to see the good stuff and imagine those people are somehow immune to the feelings of frustration and the trials and problems and griefs that you and I experience. Stop and think for a moment of a few in the public eye. Marilyn Monroe spent her life with the gnawing pain of feeling unloved, and eventually committed suicide. Howard Hughes, for all his intellect and inventive genius and money, spent the last years of his life shut off from the world in seclusion and semi darkness, with an obsession about germs. Handsome Rock Hudson died of AIDS, and the ever-cheerful Magic Johnson has the virus, too. John Belushi died of a drug overdose, as have so many others. Comedian Johnny Carson suffered the pain of failed marriages and the tragic death of a son he loved dearly. The storybook marriage of Prince Charles and Princess Diana has problems, also. We know for certain that the tabloid reporters have made it a living hell for them. So you see the rich and famous, the talented and important people are not immune from the real problems of real life. Anyone still want to sign up?

The story from 2 Kings for today is about a man named Naaman who was famous in his time. He was commanding general of the greatest army in the world — the army of Syria (or Aram), the superpower of its day. At his word people jumped to do his bidding. He could have just about anything he wanted, or could command that it be done or brought. He had everything — everything, that is, except his health. You see, General Naaman had leprosy. To have leprosy in that time was a slow and terrible death sentence. Like AIDS, in the early stages only he would know. A bit later only a few others who knew him intimately would know. But eventually everybody would know. And the fear of leprosy in that time was such that those who had it were condemned to a life of isolation from all other people, and eventually to die apart from their family and loved ones. In modern times we've learned that true leprosy is not all that contagious, and that people who have it need not be sent away to leper colonies for fear of their giving it to someone else. But in that time it resulted in an unreasoned fear that condemned its victims to pain far beyond the disease itself.

I wonder what of his fame or power or fortune Naaman might have given just to have good health once again. I have sat by the bedside of quite a number of people who would have willingly bargained with anything at their disposal to regain their health. One man with lung cancer whispered, "I'd give anything just to be able to take a deep breath again."

I've heard others wish they could give anything to be free of pain, or to be able to walk again. And they probably would give anything they had for that. The problem is that when our health fails we often do give up everything we have in terms of monetary and property resources and still lose the battle. If you have not been in that position you certainly know or have heard of someone who has. That's exactly where Naaman was, in a state of desperation where he was ready to try anything — but what?

Luckily enough there was a young captive servant girl who had an idea. She knew of a certain man in Samaria who just might help. He was a religious man — a prophet named Elisha. There is nothing to indicate that Naaman had any religious inclinations of his own, but we know that when desperate enough, people are often willing to try something they might otherwise avoid. That inclination is where the term foxhole religion comes from, where in the heat of battle even the faithless turn to faith.

Naaman was lucky enough to have influence at the top — even with the king. So the king of Aram wrote a letter to the king of Israel, and gave Naaman generous gifts he thought appropriate for someone who would cure the general of his army. Off went Naaman to seek the prophet Elisha, perhaps thinking the prophet would say prayers over him, or offer a sacrifice to his God, or give him some magical curative potion. But if that was his expectation he was to be disappointed. The biblical story paints an interesting picture of Naaman wheeling up to Elisha's house in a cloud of dust with chariots and horses and soldiers. It must have been an impressive sight — at least to anyone but Elisha. Now imagine this! General Naaman, used to commanding people to come and go, or even to lay down their lives in battle, didn't even get to see the prophet. Elisha didn't even come out of his house. He sent out an intermediary with the prescription for Naaman, which was to dip seven times into the Jordan River.

In his anger borne of some arrogance Naaman was, as the saying goes, fit to be tied, and he turned away in a rage. Of all the mighty rivers he could have washed in, why the Jordan? You might wonder that, too, if you have ever seen the Jordan. While in rainy times it may flow a pretty good stream, it is not the "mighty Jordan" that a songwriter imagined, or that Sunday school illustration artists have sometimes painted. The Jordan is only a few yards wide in most places, and rather sluggish. One is not apt to be swept away by its current. So, to wade out and bathe in this torpid tributary was beneath Naaman's dignity.

It is interesting that again Naaman's help comes from a very humble source. The original idea to seek out Elisha, you remember, came from a slave girl — a servant to Naaman's wife. Now it is an ordinary soldier who brings Naaman to his senses. What is there to lose, after all? "If the prophet had commanded you to do something difficult, would you not have done it? How much more, when all he said to you was 'Wash, and be clean?' " So Naaman swallowed his pride and bathed, and to his surprise his flesh became like that of a young child. He was cured.

Mark's gospel tells a much simpler story of a man, apparently of more humble means and demeanor than mighty Naaman. This man also was a leper and came and prostrated himself at Jesus' feet and implored him to be cured. And Jesus stretched out his hand and touched him, and the leprosy left him. The prescription for his restoration to the community was deceptively simple. "Go and show yourself to the priest." The priest was the only one who could declare the man free of his leprosy. But Jesus wished the healing to carry with it a spiritual obligation, so he told the man to make the offering that Moses had commanded as testimony for his cleansing. Then contrary to Jesus' warning not to tell anybody, the man could not contain his joy over his cure and proclaimed it to everyone, so that soon Jesus could hardly go into a town because people came to him from every direction.

The two stories may seem dissimilar, except that powerful and arrogant Naaman and the man who humbly approached Jesus were both lepers. The stories are similar in that, in both cases, the lepers were put in touch with the power of God that was already there.

The stories are also similar in that both men were cured immediately. That is certainly what we want — to be cured. To be put in touch with the power of God is somehow not as specific as most of us would like. We want the tangible evidence — the cure. Naaman, you remember, had his own idea of what the prophet ought to do. So do we sometimes when we want to see something happening. "He didn't do anything for me," we hear people complain of their physicians, as though there is always something that can be done. And when there is something seriously wrong with us we don't want to see some underling! Forget whatever credentials may be on the office wall. We want to see the person at the top — the one in charge — because when we are hurting and have that feeling of desperation within us ours is the most important case there is. "I think that for me he would surely come out," said Naaman at the prophet's door. The entire focus of life narrows down to getting cured. Of course it does! We all want to be whole and healthy. But it doesn't always happen that way, and in the narrowing process we may shut out or not realize the power of God to bring healing and life to us in other ways.

If Naaman had not been cured he probably would have returned home thinking the God of Israel was powerless after all. If the Galilean leper had not been healed he might have thought Jesus a fraud, or at least not so remarkable a healer as he had heard. Both of these were success stories of the sort we like to hear. We want it to be that way for us, too. I wonder, do you suppose there were some people who came to Jesus whom he could not or at least did not cure? Did he have to tell anyone, "I'm sorry. There's nothing more I can do for you?" If we pray to God for help, or a cure, or for a certain outcome and it does not happen, do we conclude that God is powerless or not interested, or that prayer is ineffective? Or do we, perhaps, decide that there is not a God after all? If physical healing is the only thing we will settle for then we may be sadly disappointed. If the only answer to our prayers and petitions is for someone to pass his hand over the place, or discover the magical potion just in time, then we have put very narrow limits upon the power of God in our lives.

Naaman had to get down off his horse and get into the muddy river. We have to get down off the pillar of our denial to face the reality of our situation and know what is really possible. We do not live in a magical world. There are not cures for everything. The parents of one young man I know who had cancer were so convinced that the doctors didn't know everything and there had to be a cure for him, that they went to a psychic reader for answers. But eventually they had to face the sad reality that their beloved son was going to die, which he did with dignity and grace, and the inner strength and confidence from a loving God. He was released from the body of pain that had held him prisoner. While we seek every possibility for healing of our bodies, there are times when we must recognize that release we call death is the ultimate "cure" in situations where there is no hope of recovery. In our own fear of what is before us, and our desire to be healed, what we need most desperately is to be put in touch with the healing presence and love of God. We lose touch sometimes, you know. When a cataclysmic event comes into our lives — the death of a loved one, cancer, AIDS, you name it — we may find ourselves at that moment unprepared, denying, resisting, and unable to immerse ourselves in the earthy river of God's love. We need somebody. And God sends us somebody. For Naaman it was a servant girl, a concerned king, a prophet, and a common soldier. For the Galilean man, it was Jesus alone.

When I was just a young boy, my sister, 14 years older, was killed in a plane crash. Our family was devastated. My parents each tried to deal with the grief in their own way and to help each other. I remember for my father that meant keeping busy at his work. I remember one Saturday he took me out in the orchard to work with him, but several times he dissolved into tears, and we decided to head home. But on the way home he decided to go see an old woman — a long-time family friend — who lived with her daughter's family nearby. She was older than my own grandmother, and spent most of her time rocking and knitting. She was not well educated. That was considered unnecessary for most women of her generation. She spoke with a slow Alabama drawl. I remember her Bible was never very far away from her and she apparently read it often, and I remember her kind of half-humming, half-singing some religious song now and then.

We arrived and went in, and she seemed to know what to do. She held him while he poured out his grief, and then she just quietly talked to us both. Then she said a prayer, and that was it. Ever so simple, but it was enough. It wasn't what we would have liked if we had had our choice, which was the restoration of our lost loved one in our midst, but the connection was restored and the healing power of the presence of God flowed once again. Grief can sometimes stand in the way of that presence, and it takes a friend to encourage us to step down into the stream. The words of an old spiritual song encourage us, saying, "Wade in the water. Wade in the water, children."

Whatever the illness or pain or sorrow that may be affecting your life at this moment, there is help. It may not be the magical cure you would like, but it is healing to the inner life that will enable you to bear up under whatever burden you must carry. Each of us needs to know we are not alone. The love of God touches us with the same compassion as Jesus touched that man in the Galilean village. If we are out of touch with the power of God in our lives that contact can be restored, through the simple ministrations of those who care enough to sit with us, talk with us, encourage us, and love us. Those things seem deceptively simple, but they are tremendously important.

There are times when we may even be the angels of God's love to bring healing to the life of a friend. Sometimes we say that we "don't know what to do" for someone who is ill or grieving or lonely. The answer is simple. Do the simple things. Do the thing that helps you when you are in a similar situation. Share a bit of time. Bring a bit of cheer. Stop by to visit for a few minutes, but listen more than talk. And, if you can, say a prayer before you leave. The words are not so important. It is the love that makes contact. The important thing to know is that God moves through us to one another. We are channels of God's grace. We are channels of the healing stream of God for all the ills of the whole world — the illness and the pain. Don't wait for someone else. Go! We're the ones who are sent — you and I. If we don't go, who will?

And Now For Something Completely Different

At the end of a week-long retreat in a mountain camp setting a somewhat different kind of worship service was taking place. It was at the end of a day that had been set aside for introspection and talking about feelings of self-worth. There had been some discussion about how to deal with feelings of guilt and the need to feel forgiven, and how it is often easier to forgive someone else than to forgive oneself. Since this was a retreat of church people there was frequent reference to the forgiving nature of God. But now the whole day was coming to focus in a time of worship.

All the people were gathered around. They did some singing and read several portions of scripture. There was a brief talk about forgiveness — forgiving others and forgiving one's self — and the need to put aside past hurts and injustices, and guilt of things done or left undone, in order to move forward into creative living. To that end they had all come prepared. Earlier that afternoon they had done some writing about the person they wanted to become. This they saved for future reference. And on a separate page or more they had all written about things in their lives they truly wanted to put behind them — to get rid of for good, to release, to be forgiven of, and to forget. They brought this latter bit of writing with them to the service, and there was a time to look it over and think about it one last time.

Then came an offering of sorts. The people were asked to take out and read, and then wad up the pages representing the things they wanted to get out of their lives, and to place them in a large ceramic pot which someone brought around to each one. It was interesting to note that some dropped in their wadded paper thoughtfully — almost reluctantly. A few did so with some self-conscious tears. A few slammed their wad into the pottery jar with energy and determination. Then the worship leader stood before them and held aloft the heavy ceramic jar in both hands, and led the group in a prayer. The prayer was that God help banish the pain and guilt of the past, and give them strength to remove — even to "smash," as the prayer put it — all that was sinful and unworthy within them. At that point the leader dropped the heavy clay pot and it came smashing down on the stone floor with a resounding crash and broke into dozens of pieces. People who had had their eyes closed now had them wide open. The prayer seemed to sputter on for a couple short sentences, but for the most part that sound had ended it. There was a physical reaction on the part of everyone there. They had been startled wide-eyed awake by the noise and the visual impact of the broken pot. It was a shocking and dramatic moment, and it took a moment for everyone to know what it meant. Then they understood! That crash was supposed to symbolize a turning point or a departure, and it was meant to be remembered.

After the momentary shock a man from the back row said a resounding, "Aw-right!" A quiet older lady tried not to be timid and ventured a "Hooray!" A couple of people applauded. And then the whole group put aside their timidity and began to applaud and stood up, smiling and nodding to one another. A few people exchanged hugs. There was another song or so and a closing prayer and they all went out into the night, apparently feeling somewhat lighter and happier. Perhaps some felt relieved. It had been a mountaintop experience to remember and treasure.

"Behold, I am doing a new thing, do you not perceive it?" With images that do not seem to go together, Deutero-Isaiah

106

sets out an agenda of the unexpected for people who expected nothing. Imagine it, even the beasts giving praise to God — beasts as different as the jackal and the ostrich! Now there's an unlikely combination. There will be streams in the desert — hardly a place one would expect to find refreshing water to drink. And the Lord proclaims refreshing drink to those still called chosen people, despite the fact they haven't behaved much like chosen people.

You see, at one time God did choose these Israelites, and they chose God, and there was a covenant between them. But then they became unfaithful to the covenant. And now they have gone off looking for fulfillment everywhere else, and have ignored even the smallest praise of God. There's a contemporary image for you. And that is not all. The Lord says, "You have burdened me with your sins; you have wearied me with your iniquities." (Isaiah 43:24) Then comes the surprise. "I, I am he who blots out your transgressions for my own sake, and I will not remember your sins." (Isaiah 43:25)

Is something missing? Is there a step left out? Is this some kind of a trick? Is Isaiah, speaking for the Lord, declaring forgiveness before repentance? Yes! Of course we've always assumed it works the other way around, and there are plenty of scriptural precedents for saying it that way, and it is certainly the way we prefer to practice it — repentance first and then forgiveness. "Don't forgive him until he is truly sorry." And we might add, "And I'm really going to make him sorry!" One reason we tend to hold back our forgiveness is because we see it as a weapon — a way to get even. So we turn around our hurt as a poisoned dart to strike back. But putting aside the tendency to get even, another reason we tend to reserve our forgiveness of another is that it seems like giving up something of ourselves. It does indeed demand something of us, to climb down from our pedestal to humility. Think for a moment of the drama of two children glaring at each other through teary eyes as a mother requires one to say, "I'm sorry," and the other to say, "You're forgiven," or words to that effect. Both are reluctant, to apologize or to forgive.

That mother/father God-image is a good one for us to remember, standing over us and trying to bring about some reconciliation to allow us to get on with life. But the order of the transaction is not always the same. Forgiveness is a risky thing. We fear it may not always be deserved. Of course if forgiveness were always deserved we would likely not do much forgiving. To forgive even prior to another's repentance may get the forgiver involved more deeply with the forgivee than was either anticipated or desired at first.

On a daytime talk show some time ago, a couple was interviewed whose daughter had been killed in an auto accident. The accident was the fault of a drunk driver. Grief over the daughter's death almost destroyed her parents as well. The man whose fault it was went to trial and was sentenced to prison. That's the justice we all would probably want to see, as did those grieving parents. But here is where the scenario breaks with the expected and becomes something entirely new and different. Of course no words of remorse on the guilty man's part could bring back the lovely young girl he had killed but he said them anyhow. Nor could any amount of anger and grief on the parents' part change what had happened. During the trial they watched him, seeing how his own grief at what his irresponsibility had done was changing his own life as well. As they watched and listened they became aware that they were seeing another life disintegrating before their very eyes. It was then that the compassion borne out of their Christian faith overwhelmed their anger and tempered their sorrow. To everyone's surprise, and even their own, they went to visit this young man in jail. It was a tense meeting at first as you might expect, especially on his part. Despite their immense grief these two parents were able to express not only their concern for him, but the fact that they had already forgiven him for what he had done. While nothing could ever erase from his mind the memory of what he had done to their daughter and to them, he was forgiven by them.

They continued to visit him during his entire prison term, and in time they came to care for and even love him. Imagine that! When the young man was let out of prison they invited him to visit them, and he even stayed with them, as he tried to put together the shattered pieces of his life. They helped him get into an alcohol abuse treatment program. Later on he began to go to church with them. In time he came to be regarded almost as a member of their family, incredible as that seems. But then, true forgiveness often involves us more deeply in the life of the one forgiven than we anticipate. Perhaps fear of that involvement is another reason we sometimes withhold it.

This man appeared on that show with the two parents and told how their love helped him to conquer his drinking problem, and expressed to all who heard him his continual amazement at the power of forgiving love. I dare say that talk show touched more people with the incredible power of the forgiveness of God through people than any church service. "Behold, I am doing a new thing." Do you perceive it? Can you imagine it? "I am he who blots out your transgressions for my own sake, and I will not remember your sins," not because you deserve it, or even ask for it, but "for my own sake." (Isaiah 43:25)

We need to forgive for our own sake, too. Otherwise it festers within us. We have to get rid of it, cleanse our inner being and get on with our life. Strange, but true, the hardest person to forgive is oneself. We all know people who go around heaped with guilt for real or imagined wrongs committed against someone, or things of which they are ashamed. We may have experienced to some degree the debilitating weight of the ever-present nagging guilt we cannot seem to shake off. We all must find a way to put the past behind us and leave it there. Not that we will forget. Certainly we hope we will learn from experience — even bad experience — but we must not let it unravel our life.

A sailor, writing of the pleasures and hazards of sailing small pleasure boats, told of the choice that faces one whose craft is wrecked within sight of land. There are two choices. One is to stay there and cling to the wreckage, hoping someone may eventually see and come to the rescue. The other choice is to let go and strike out for shore. Either choice has its risks. One may cling to the wreckage and never be found, and perhaps drift farther out to sea. On the other hand, in attempting to swim to shore there is the possibility one may become exhausted, or get muscle cramps, and drown. But he said that if he had a reasonable chance his option would always be to try to reach the shore, because that is where life goes on. The unfortunate thing is that too many people choose to cling to whatever wreckage there is in their lives, failing to see that by doing so they are drifting farther and farther from life's possibilities.

There are various ways of trying to let go of the wreckage in the will to choose life. We may only need the encouragement and advice of a good friend, or perhaps a compassionate pastor. Sometimes it is more complicated than that and we need to seek the help of a trained and skilled counselor to help us. In any case the point must be that we must get to the place where we can forgive ourselves and move onto the mainland of living once again.

Jesus understood the disabling effect of feeling unforgiven — by God, or by someone else, or even by oneself. As his popularity was growing, people crowded in upon him. On one such occasion there were so many people crowded around and in the house where he was that nobody could get near, and yet he taught those who came to him. A few clever people had a man who was paralyzed whom they wanted to get into the very presence of Jesus. The fact he was paralyzed is a good analogy for our own situation whereby we are often paralyzed in a spiritual or psychological sense, though not often in a physical sense, by the guilt we carry.

Now imagine this scene! Those people took apart part of the roof of the house, and with ropes lowered the paralyzed man down to Jesus. Jesus saw the opportunity to do something completely different from what they had heard from him. He said to the man, "Your sins are forgiven." But the people who heard him say that could not comprehend the new thing God was doing through Jesus in that new concept. They questioned, and Jesus explained, "Which is easier, to say 'Your sins are forgiven,' or to say 'Rise up and pick up your bed and walk?' " (Mark 2:9) So he said it in the manner of a healer, which they could accept but which was equally valid! They understood the new equation. What difference does it make when a person is released from the devastating effects of this sinfulness they feel, whether it is the result of the treatment of a psychiatrist or psychologist or a pastoral counselor or some other means. Nor do we have to put a religious label upon a thing in order for God to be working through it. For God is doing a new thing, and it may be such as we have never seen before. The part that faith plays in all this is that even before we feel the forgiveness of another person, or are able to forgive ourselves, we are already forgiven by God. "I, I am he who blots out your transgressions. . . I will not remember your sins." And if God will not remember them, it is time for us to let them be in the past and look forward.

There are a couple simple techniques that, as a counselor, I sometimes suggest with therapy, especially if one needs to resolve problems from the past involving people who are no longer around. One is to get away alone to someplace for a day or two for a personal retreat — for relaxation and enjoyment and thought. What I suggest is that the person spend at least part of the time writing in a notebook about the things that we've discovered together that are unresolved. The writing may consist of letters to someone who is already dead — maybe a parent or sister or brother or friend — with whom there are still some unresolved issues. The letter is to say the things you wish you had been able to say to bring about resolution and forgiveness and reconciliation. Or you may write a narrative, or just notes, about the painful unresolved problems from the past; perhaps about feelings of inadequacy, or regrets for deeds done or opportunities missed. The letters and notes are not for sending in the usual sense. They are to be written, and read, and perhaps prayed about, and then destroyed. Yet, it is much like that worship service mentioned earlier, and with the same intent. Make a ceremony of it. Put

111

them into a fire one by one, or into a paper shredder if you wish, though that can sometimes take on its own particular symbolism. It ought to be a ceremony that bespeaks finality. Then at the end of each such experience, and certainly at the end of the retreat, do something to celebrate. How you celebrate is not important, so long as for you it really is celebration.

The other technique is for those who prefer to be more verbal, and whose minds may not be patient with the tediousness of writing. Of course one needs to get away to a place where, if anyone hears, they won't wonder about someone who is talking and carrying on conversations when nobody else is there. We may talk to ourselves at other times, but when we do it in earnest and with a purpose people who overhear tend to become a bit uneasy. The technique is to talk out what we want to leave behind, and if this means talking to the people who are no longer with us — declaring your love, asking forgiveness, giving it — then do that. Don't do it for benefit of a tape recorder. You don't want to save this stuff, so don't record it. You want to get it behind you, and to leave it in the past.

"Behold I am doing a new thing; do you see it?" Can you understand it? Can you accept it? Yes, even you who have looked for life's fulfillment in all the wrong places. Even you who have gone far away from God. Even you who have wearied the Lord by loose and careless and hurtful and sinful living. Even you! Even me! To us the message is the same. The One who has the power to erase the guilt of all our transgressions tells us "I will not [even] remember your sins." Now, that's good news! How's that for something different and new and wonderful? We can jettison the wreckage from our lives and swim free toward new life. We can arise from our paralytic bed and go home. And seeing the change, people about us may be amazed, and they may even glorify God, and say, "We never saw anything like this."

The Scandal Of
Redeeming Love

It seems that we have developed a tabloid mentality. That is to say, we seem to have developed an overzealous fascination for information about the private lives of public people. The real or supposed exploits of actors and actresses, politicians, entertainers, athletes or business moguls appear in lurid headlines on papers and magazines that are more interested in sensation than news. Photographers stalk the rich or famous to catch an image of an unguarded moment. Fact blended with fiction becomes the means to enhance or discredit; to glorify or defame. The popularity of this material in tabloid papers, magazines and talk shows indicates that the public seems to have an insatiable appetite for it. Probably most of the subjects of the scandal and gossip, half-truth and innuendo would far rather be left alone than to see their names and pictures, and the supposed details of their lives, paraded before the public.

The prophet Hosea, however, used the painfully lurid details of his own personal life to reach people. It was an attention grabber all right. If there had been copies on the newsstands, so to speak, one can imagine them being grabbed off by the gossip-seekers. The story told by Hosea himself is that he married Gomer, a woman with a past, to put it politely. To put it not so politely, she was a prostitute. She probably plied her trade in connection with the Caananite fertility cult of the Baal gods which used prostitutes as a form of worship. But Hosea loved Gomer and their marriage covenant provided her a new beginning — a new life — and he took her away from that past. Gomer became his wife. There were children, too, but here some other issues are raised, as to whether they were even Hosea's offspring or not. Can you imagine the headlines over all this? But there is still more to come.

Gomer apparently got tired of the marriage and left Hosea, and returned to the life of a prostitute. Hosea urged the children to plead with their mother to return, but she did not. Eventually Hosea found Gomer in a slave market and bought her freedom — redeemed her — and declaring his love for her took her home once again to be his wife.

It is at once a shocking and a beautiful story. It is shocking in the painful revelations of domestic tragedy that it portrays. It is beautiful in that it expresses a love that redeems. One can imagine that those reading it would think Hosea had been foolish in taking Gomer as his wife in the first place, let alone buying her at the slave market and taking her as his wife a second time. Perhaps in their eyes what they saw as Hosea's apparent foolishness and poor judgment would even disqualify him as a prophet of the Lord. Hosea was sure the match was one, if not made in heaven, at least still bound by a sacred covenant, and more than that by his love for Gomer. Surely it was after the full force of his marital troubles struck him that he began to see in it how he imagined God must feel at Israel's failure to fulfill its part of the covenant with Yahweh.

Hosea was not a professional prophet by any means. In fact he was a farmer who liked to write poetry. The book of Hosea, as we have it, represents several of these poems which he may have written on the road, on marketing trips to Samaria and Jezreel. One often has a lot of time to think on a long trip. And Hosea had quite a lot to think about, considering the sad state of his home life, and the equally sad state of the nation. He apparently saw some striking similarities, and put his prophecy in the form of poems designed to call people back to their obligations of their covenant with Yahweh. Lest anyone doubt the power of poetry to move people, Bible historians hold that Hosea's prophetic work was instrumental in saving Israel from absorption into the Baal cults, the indigenous sexually-oriented fertility cult religion of the Caananites, which would have meant the loss of the very thing that distinguished the Israelites as a people.

The one thing that set Israel apart from all the other peoples around them was their covenant with Yahweh. That Israel would break that covenant surely must have pained Yahweh, in the same way that Gomer's breaking of the marriage covenant pained him. Hosea saw in Yahweh a God of infinite love, who loved Israel despite its disobedience, and who would no less pursue and redeem Israel than Hosea pursued and redeemed Gomer as his wife.

A covenant, of course, is an agreement of mutual benefit whereby each party agrees to certain obligations. Covenants were the legal arrangements which made society work, and by which peaceful relationships were established between peoples and tribes, and even individuals. Deals were struck and a covenant arrived at, and there were often symbols that were to serve as reminders. Sometimes tokens were exchanged — as a wedding ring is used today — to symbolize that covenant. But in those days a cairn of rocks might be set up, or a single large stone, and even anointed as a witness, or a sacrifice might be made to formalize the sacred vows that constituted the covenant.

Israel was bound to Yahweh not just loosely and casually, but by a covenant, whereby Yahweh chose Israel to be his people, and Israel in turn chose Yahweh to be its God. Keeping the covenant with God, or failing to keep it, was the determinant of prosperity, of life or death, of blessing or curse. The scripture narrative is essentially the story of the fortunes of the people in regard to how faithful they were to that sacred covenant. So anything from drought and failure of crops, to defeat in battle and captivity by another nation, was attributed in some way to Israel's unfaithfulness to Yahweh. Likewise

Israel at its best was interpreted as due to its faithfulness and righteousness before the Lord.

When the prophet Hosea came upon the scene about 740 B.C.E., things were becoming rather chaotic. The nation's unity and prosperity had given way to factionalism and conflict, and even civil war. The fragmented and weakened nation, then, was a sitting duck for Assyria in its westward campaigns. Hosea was much saddened by this turn of events. He was sure that it was because Israel had turned away from the holy covenant with Yahweh, and put its trust in alliances and might. Just as Gomer had abandoned him, he saw that Israel was abandoning Yahweh, so he tried to unify and save his nation, principally by calling the people back to the covenant. The dramatic means he chose to gain attention was by the revelation of his own very painful domestic tragedy.

It was that tragedy which so deeply affected his own life that became the means of insight into what he supposed were the feelings of Yahweh toward the faithless nation of Israel. Gomer abandoned him, but he continued to love her through the pain of feeling deserted. Thus he posited the idea that Yahweh's love for Israel would cause him to seek and redeem and restore Israel.

> Therefore, I will now allure her,
>   and bring her into the wilderness,
>   and speak tenderly to her.
> From there I will give her vineyards,
>   and make the Valley of Achor a door of hope.
> Then she shall respond as in the days of her youth,
>   as at the time when she came out of the land of Egypt.
>   — Hosea 2:14-15

The promise is that the remembrance of the sins of the past, symbolized by the reference to the Valley of Achor, will not be an eternal reminder of the sins of the past, but a door of hope. Achor, you remember, was the place where, upon entering the Promised Land, Israel sinned and acted contrary to the word of the Lord. (Joshua 7:20-26) Hosea hopes, then, that Israel will realize its faithlessness and return to Yahweh, and be faithful to the covenant. Again he uses the image of marriage.

> On that day, says the Lord, you will call me, "My husband," and no longer you will call me, "My Baal," for I will remove the names of the Baals from her mouth, and they shall be mentioned by name no more. I will make for you a covenant on that day with the wild animals, the birds of the air, and the creeping things of the ground; and I will abolish the bow, the sword, and war from the land; and I will make you lie down in safety. And I will take you for my wife forever; I will take you for my wife in righteousness and in justice, in steadfast love, and in mercy. I will take you for my wife in faithfulness; and you shall know the Lord.
> — Hosea 2:16-20

Here, a poetic prophet 750 years before the time of Jesus, reveals his own painful marital woes before the people in order to also reveal a God of infinite love. The foolishness that some might have perceived in Hosea, in continuing to love his wayward wife, illustrates the wonderful love of God, whose love is not shortened by human disobedience. That love still extended to Israel in its abrogation of the covenant relationship, and even when it abandoned Yahweh, whoring after the pagan Baal gods. And the love of Yahweh would even redeem Israel from the lowest degradation, to be restored again in the family, and the covenant renewed. That is the very theme that Jesus portrayed in the parable about a prodigal son. The so-called foolishness of God is love that knows no limits.

Jesus portrayed in his life this loving and redeeming God. Mark's gospel, in the reading for today, tells first of Jesus teaching by the sea, and then as he passed by the place where Levi the son of Alphaeus was sitting and collecting taxes, Jesus said to him, "Follow me," and Levi rose and followed him.

117

That Jesus would call such a man to follow him was scandalous in itself, for Levi was a renegade Jew. That is, he was one who deliberately chose to separate himself from the Jewish community and become a collaborator with the Roman occupation forces, serving as a tax collector. It was a way of getting rich, and we are familiar with the fact that principles and ideals are often compromised for personal gain. In the understanding of the Judaism of the time he had knowingly separated himself from the precepts of the covenant, and add to that what they saw as disloyalty to Israel, and for all of that there was no forgiveness. He was hated and shunned by the Jews. But Jesus came along and called him away from that, saying, "Follow me!" And in that call, and Levi's response, is the very incarnation of forgiveness and redemption. The clear implication to Levi was, "Your sins are forgiven." For Levi, at that very moment, there was a new covenant in force. The very thing which he did not deserve, he received as a pure, unconditional, and unqualified gift of God.

The gospel, though, is not just a "once-upon-a-time" story. It is contemporary. It is the context in which we can behold what is available now, to each one of us. What happened to Levi can happen to anyone. The story of Levi is an invitation to follow Jesus and receive the new life that is offered to us.

Jesus apparently went home with Levi, and there in his house he ate with Levi and some of his friends — other tax collectors. Shunned by the Jewish community, the tax collectors had only themselves with whom to associate. Of course Jesus was roundly criticized by the righteous Pharisees and scribes for eating with tax collectors and sinners. In fact, these persons were not just distasteful for what they did, but were considered cultically unclean. In other words, they were unfit for God's community. For Jesus to sit at table with such people, in the Pharisees' view, was to defile himself.

The human tendency is to divide people from one another. Though not stated in the terms my high school English teacher would approve, we divide people into categories of them and us. Like the Pharisees of Jesus' time, who divided people between the righteous and the sinners, clean and unclean, Jew and Gentile, we do the same thing. One of the sad commentaries on our own day is that we continue to build more walls of separation than bridges of acceptance. Like those Pharisees even good church people can come to believe they have a corner on truth and goodness, and that others, by reason of belief, or race, or sexual orientation, or a host of other reasons, are somehow less worthy and less acceptable in the community of faith. In every age, even good people are blinded by their own self-righteousness and deafened by their own self-protectiveness.

Jesus on the other hand, in sitting at a meal with those people, erased those commonly held lines of distinction. The new covenant operates on an entirely new assumption, that there is no such thing as ritual uncleanness, but that we all have in our own way been unfaithful. "The kingdom of God is at hand," said Jesus, and forgiveness is the sign that the new order — the new covenant — is already present and operating, and so new patterns of behavior are mandatory.

The ancient prophet Hosea declared that God's love would redeem the people, from the forces of rebellion and disobedience. Jesus declared that all people — even the hated tax collectors and sinners, and any other category you want to name — are offered forgiveness and entry into the kingdom. Judgment and grace operate together in this new order. Judgment declares that all have fallen short of the glory of God, and grace offers the gift of undeserved forgiveness. Jesus ate with Levi and his friends because God's grace included all of them. When people come to church to receive the sacrament of the Lord's supper that same idea is at work. We do not receive Christ because we deserve to do so, but because we do not deserve to, and not because we are righteous, but because we recognize our need to be forgiven.

Jesus' enigmatic statement that, "Those who are well have no need of a physician, but those who are sick; I came not to call the righteous, but sinners," should raise questions in our minds, as undoubtedly it did in the minds of the Pharisees.

Just who are those righteous ones, and who are the sinners? At first glance the distinction may seem clear, but upon closer examination we must confess there is no clear distinction at all. Jesus shares the meal with sinners because there is nobody else. Nobody is excluded from his presence except those who choose to exclude themselves.

The idea of the out-reaching, forgiving and redeeming love that was planted as a seed by Hosea found its full growth and flower in Jesus. Hosea risked the ridicule and embarrassment of public scrutiny of his personal life to reveal the aspect of love that was to become the foundation of the new covenant. Jesus risked the criticism of the Pharisees, and eventually gave up his life in showing the extent to which the love of God reaches, even to people who despise and reject him. That we are invited to accept that love and live as people of the new covenant is cause for joy. Hosea promised that the Valley of Achor would become a door of hope for a whole people. Jesus opens the door of the kingdom wide and bids everyone enter. Yes, even those avoided and shunned and condemned by pharisaic self-righteousness. Wherever and whoever we are, Jesus offers new life not just patched up with the religious legalisms and practices of the past, but completely made new, and as effervescent as new wine.

Coming Down
The Mountain

There is a story that a university in Scotland once wished to honor a scholar who had done some significant inquiry into the life and work of one of its own most illustrious former scholars, the 16th century Scottish reformer, John Knox. The tradition in that and several other universities was that, if possible, a cap belonging to the subject of the study — in this case John Knox — would be given to the person being honored, if such a cap could be found. In that way the honoree would have something personal, imbued at least in thought, by a sense of the man who had once worn it. But the only cap of John Knox that anyone knew about had already been presented to someone else years before. However the university did possess a pair of trousers that had once belonged to Knox, so they had a cap made from its material and presented it to the scholar who, though surely amused, was undoubtedly grateful to have received anything actually owned by that reformer and theologian.

Such symbols, and often rather humble ones at that, are important because they connect us to people who are important to us. Indeed in some cases authority is inherited with a symbol denoting ownership, or in some countries, the right to a title. The reading for today from 2 Kings tells of the apprentice prophet Elisha who inherited the mantle — a sleeveless cloak

— that had been worn by his aged mentor, the prophet Elijah, and had come to be symbolic of his authority as a prophet of God.

The power and greatness of Elijah always seem to be expressed in terms of legends and miracles. One of these legends is inferred at the very beginning of today's reading, that Elijah would not die as ordinary mortals do. Rather, like Enoch before him, he was to be taken up to heaven in a whirlwind. What a way to go, and it wasn't even in Kansas!

Apparently that impending event was no secret. It seemed well known among the company of prophets, or the members of the prophetic order that came out to meet Elijah and Elisha along the way. In fact they came out to warn Elisha that his mentor, Elijah, was about to be taken away from him. But apparently Elisha was also aware of what was about to happen. It is clear that he had no intention of letting Elijah out of his sight. Despite Elijah telling him at several points on the way to wait while he went on ahead, Elisha stayed close at hand. Almost at the last minute the old prophet asked Elisha what he wanted from him before he departed. Elisha's answer was "a double portion of your spirit." Now while the request was a compliment to the old prophet, in the end Elisha apparently did not receive that "double portion," but he received something else, and perhaps something more important. As they were walking along suddenly a chariot and horses of fire came between them, and Elijah was swept up in the whirlwind and his mantle dropped to the ground.

The story beyond today's reading goes on to tell us that Elisha picked up the mantle and went back to the Jordan River they had crossed together earlier. Elisha struck the water of the river with Elijah's mantle just as the old prophet had done earlier, and the waters parted, and Elisha crossed over. The crossing of the Jordan was, symbolically, the Rubicon which separated the apprentice or assistant that he had been, to become in his own right the prophet of God.

So Elijah was gone. Elisha had assumed his mantle and the authority it symbolized. The parted waters even attested that he now had the powers of his now departed mentor. The other prophets who saw Elisha return recognized his new authority. After these prophets searched in vain for three days for the body of the old man, they returned and asked Elisha to use his new powers to sweeten a well which theretofore had only brought forth bad water and sickness and poor crops. So Elisha went to work and became the prophet of the Lord in the midst of the people, as Elijah had been before him. Today, by tradition, the finest spring in Jericho is sometimes called Elisha's Fountain.

A tradition based upon the legend of Elijah's departure from earth in the whirlwind is that the prophet would return to earth before the Messiah would appear. In fact, a tradition among the Jews at Passover is to set a place at the table, but leave it empty for Elijah, or perhaps an unexpected or needy guest, and the door is left open a crack for the same reason. The tradition that Elijah would return as a presager of the Messiah provides a bridge to another important scripture for today from Mark's gospel.

A few days after Jesus had told the disciples of his impending suffering, and of the way and cost of his own discipleship, he took three of his closest friends among the disciples — Peter, James and John — to a high mountain apart from anyone else. While they were there they had a remarkable vision of Jesus in which he was transfigured before them. That is to say they saw him in what we might call a non-earthly appearance, and dazzlingly bright. In the vision they saw Jesus talking with Moses, the law-giver, and Elijah, the prophet. Clearly Mark is telling us this vision has messianic significance, the symbolism of which would not be lost upon the disciples, nor upon the Christians of the Markan tradition whose belief about Jesus it represented. The vision is to attest to who Jesus is — the Messiah, the Christ.

In Matthew's and Luke's accounts Peter says to Jesus, "it is good for us to be here," seeming to imply that it would also be good to stay. Peter would like to have commemorated the moment — held it there if he could, despite his fear — by building three booths, one each for Jesus and Moses and Elijah. Then at the end of the vision, as they were about to descend from the mountain, a voice came from the clouds saying, "This is my son, the Beloved; listen to him!"

Have you ever been on such a wonderful emotional high you wished it would never end? Perhaps you remember the euphoria after a spectacular concert, or a summer camp, or a very moving religious retreat, or a memorable time with someone very important to you. How we would like to capture those moments and make them last forever. How we wish we could remain on the level of an enlightened moment, or a time of emotional or spiritual sensitivity that seems to come to us so rarely. Such times can be the touchstones of a new awakening in us, to be recalled later with some nostalgia as bright moments never completely dimmed by time. We want to cling to them, preserve them, and recreate them if possible. But the realities of life do not allow us to continue to live at that peak level all the time. In fact those high points of our experience probably stand out in bold relief against where we do live most of the time. Those singular moments; those times of inspiration and enlightenment, of joy and enthusiasm not only add zest to life, but they also give it direction and meaning.

A reading of the gospels will reveal that for the disciples themselves there was no other comparable revelatory and visionary experience while Jesus was with them. And in this one only three of the 12 were involved. The other nine only heard of it, presumably, by word of mouth tinged with the enthusiasm of Peter, James and John. Yes, the gospels tell of healings and of Jesus teaching and feeding multitudes of people, but nowhere else do they have such an emotionally charged experience as those three with Jesus on the mountaintop that day, until the Spirit came upon them at Pentecost. Rather the gospels tell us of the daily work of Jesus and the disciples, going from place to place on the dusty roads to teach and preach. They tell of conflicts with local village elders, and criticism from the religious establishment, and the friction of differing ideas. Luckily some give us a few of the teaching parables of Jesus. But for the most part it is everyday routine, but nevertheless energy-consuming activities — crowds of people, teaching, ministering to individual needs — from which Jesus and the disciples tried to get away alone for a brief time of quietness. So while the disciples were with Jesus, learning from him and witnessing the things he did, the gospels do not indicate a life of constant excitement and euphoria.

Most ministers hear complaints from time to time from people who ask, "Why isn't the church more exciting?" I've never been really sure what people mean by that. Certainly the church may seem pretty dull to people who are in search of excitement. Contrary to the enjoyable fiction perpetuated in films from "Going My Way" to "Sister Act," excitement is not something that is "produced," as though it were a function of the songs we sing, nor by an evangelistic style of preaching, or decoration of churches with banners, or hand-pumping or hugging friendliness. Those may all have their place. The assumption underlying the question seems to be that whenever we worship together it ought to be highly charged with emotion. We need to recognize that there are as many people turned off by that approach as there are attracted by it. Also it is impossible to maintain a high emotional level, or to re-create it over and over, Sunday after Sunday if, indeed, that were important. This is not to diminish the fact that the church always needs new ideas and material, and needs to seize upon the inherent drama of the good news in worship. At the other end of the spectrum the Friends (Quakers) have discovered the Spirit's presence in simple calm quietness, perhaps because they have cultivated to a rather high degree the ability to listen to the inner spirit, or to the voice of God.

There are renewal movements and retreats and the like in our churches from time to time. Given wise leadership and realistic expectations they can be very beneficial. The church always needs new ideas and a new infusion of spirit. There is a danger, however, when people return and, with disappointment in their voices and some disillusionment about the church that sent them, declare, "Why can't the church be like that?"

125

Well, maybe it could be if an occasional week-end retreat was all it did. Retreats are often rarified atmosphere. They are designed to be mountaintop experiences, composed of a select group of people who are going with a special purpose and perhaps prepared with some expectations, and away from the pressures of everyday life, with a program that can be recycled for each new group that comes. That's not what the local church does. The committee meetings, and Sunday school teacher recruitment, and financing the church program, and keeping the buildings in shape are not generally very inspiring stuff. Teaching a class of little children, or conducting a choir rehearsal with key people missing, or teaching a class of adults who were out too late the night before is hard work. So is dealing with grief, and counseling people with marital problems, and standing beside the bed of a dying friend, and calling on people who are lonely. We don't have an abundance of volunteers for these kinds of things. When I hear someone say, "Why isn't the church more exciting?" I usually conclude that the person who says it may be somewhat out of touch with what the church is doing on an everyday basis.

It is true, the church generally doesn't do a very good job of being exciting, at least in terms of emotional appeal. It is good when we can appeal to people in such a way that they feel taken to the mountaintop, and experience a time of special spiritual awareness or enlightenment, or even conversion. But then we need to hear, as the disciples heard, "This is my son, the Beloved; listen to him!" Our best efforts at renewal are not in tinkering with structure and worship, or messing with people's emotions, but in cultivating the ability to hear the word of Jesus, and then to do it.

John Wesley was a powerful dynamo of spiritual power who started a movement that profoundly changed a nation and produced a body of followers, but he records only one such dramatic moment in his own life. It wasn't in church either, but in a little meeting house on Aldersgate Street in London, where, by his own admission, he went very unwillingly. In what we might call a study group today, someone was reading a tract by Martin Luther, called "Preface to the Epistle to the Romans." Not very dramatic material, it would seem, but Luther's words concerning "the change that God works in the heart through faith in Christ," touched Wesley deeply and he felt his heart "strangely warmed." Still rather tame, as mountaintop experiences go. Not the kind of thing people mean when they want the church to be more exciting. But for Wesley, it was enough, and it is the moment he cites in his journal when he was sure of his own salvation, and is surely the critical experience that inspired a lifetime of social action and teaching and preaching. Yet Wesley never again mentions another experience that even comes close to that one. This drama of the soul and its life-long effect reached John Wesley through the intellect, and the Spirit of that encounter accompanied him throughout his life. It was no vision, as for those three disciples, but a more ordinary inspiration that dawns upon the spirit through the intellect, of the sort that you or I might have when in our quest to know the power of God in our own lives we come to a moment where we say, "Aha!" and realize that our spirit has been touched profoundly, perhaps by something we have read or heard, or a thought that suddenly becomes clear.

Martin Luther King, Jr. underlined his impassioned message of civil rights claiming "I've been to the mountaintop." Wherever and whenever that high encounter with God took place in his life, it sent him back down into the cities and streets, into the ghettos and the poor rural areas. It sent him to city hall and to Washington, to the Birmingham jail, and to Selma — and to Memphis. He didn't have to continually re-create the encounter. He continued to listen to the word of Jesus, and that was enough.

Mark tells us that when Jesus and the disciples started back down to the valley, Jesus asked them not to talk about the vision they had on the mountain, at least not until after his resurrection. Of course as yet they had no idea what that meant. But it was probably good advice anyhow. We sometimes tend to talk too much about the things we understand least. Neither did they go down to the other disciples and tell them they must

127

try to have the same experience. Some people tend to over-validate their own very personal religious experiences and think that others must have them as well. But Jesus' counsel to them was to be quiet until a later and perhaps more appropriate time. Perhaps for the other disciples, as for most of us, there would be less dramatic but just as valid revelations and inspirations.

Peter and the others, who would have liked to have lingered and enjoyed the high place of the theophanous vision a bit longer, were nevertheless led back down to the valley. There was a group of people awaiting them, and there had been some controversy. Doesn't it seem as though that's the way it always happens? One is brought back to reality rather abruptly. I know that for me it has happened sometimes after a particularly fine and moving worship service that I want to savor for a while, that someone has greeted me with some need that I must attend to, or a complaint that I must hear. We want to stay a bit longer in our enjoyment of a meaningful moment, but the needs of the world await us.

The needs of the world that awaited Jesus and his disciples were focused in a father who had brought his young son to be healed. I remember seeing an artist's depiction of the scene. There is the mountain — the scene of the magnificent messianic vision — and there are Jesus and the three disciples descending the path. At the bottom are the father and son, with others around them awaiting for Jesus. That's the way life must be also, with the heights of inspiration painted on the same canvas as the valleys where we live and serve. They are part of the same thing, and can never be very far apart.

The high and revelatory moments of life come to us in various ways. A few are fortunate to experience very dramatic high moments of illumination and exaltation. For others of us those high moments of illumination are, like Wesley's, more quiet and inward. But it is when we encounter the presence of Christ that we have the chance to view life from a new perspective, with luminous vision and clarity. And then, like Elisha coming back across the Jordan, and Jesus and his disciples coming down the mountain, we are brought back to the world of human encounter.

Yes, we've been to the mountaintop! We've been with Jesus! We have seen a vision, and we'll never be the same. We even have someone to show us the way to serve and love, for the admonition to the disciples is to us as well, "This is my son, the Beloved; listen to him." Where we are called to live is the valley of everyday life and to bring the light and clarity of our vision with us, and the vision God gives us is enough to illumine every encounter.

Lord, you have indeed sent somebody to help! You have sent us!

Books In This Cycle B Series

Gospel Set

Christmas Is A Quantum Leap
Sermons For Advent, Christmas And Epiphany
Glenn Schoonover

From Dusk To Dawn
Sermons For Lent And Easter
C. Michael Mills

The Spirit's Tether
Sermons For Pentecost (First Third)
Leonard H. Budd

Assayings: Theological Faith Testings
Sermons For Pentecost (Middle Third)
Robert L. Salzgeber

Spectators Or Sentinels?
Sermons For Pentecost (Last Third)
Arthur H. Kolsti

First Lesson Set

Why Don't You Send Somebody?
Sermons For Advent, Christmas And Epiphany
Frederick C. Edwards

The Power To Change
Sermons For Lent And Easter
Durwood L. Buchheim

The Way Of The King
Sermons For Pentecost (First Third)
Charles Curley

The Beginning Of Wisdom
Sermons For Pentecost (Middle Third)
Sue Anne Steffey Morrow

Daring To Hope
Sermons For Pentecost (Last Third)
John P. Rossing